LUXURY APARTMENT HOUSES OF MANHATTAN

AN ILLUSTRATED HISTORY

ANDREW ALPERN

DOVER PUBLICATIONS, INC.
New York

Published in Canada by General Publishing Company, Ltd., 30 Lesmill Road, Don Mills, Toronto, Ontario.
Published in the United Kingdom by Constable and Company, Ltd., 3 The Lanchesters, 162–164 Fulham Palace Road, London W6 9ER.

Luxury Apartment Houses of Manhattan: An Illustrated History is a new work, first published by Dover Publications, Inc., in 1992.

Manufactured in the United States of America
Dover Publications, Inc., 31 East 2nd Street, Mineola, N.Y. 11501

Library of Congress Cataloging-in-Publication Data

Alpern, Andrew.
    Luxury apartment houses of Manhattan : an illustrated history / by Andrew Alpern.
        p.   cm.
    Includes index.
    ISBN 0-486-27370-9
    1. Apartment houses—New York (N.Y.)—History. 2. Upper classes—New York (N.Y.)—Dwellings—History. 3. New York (N.Y.)—Buildings, structures, etc.—History. 4. Manhattan (New York, N.Y.)—Buildings, structures, etc.—History. I. Title.
NA7860.A498 1992
728′.314′097471—dc20   92-26286
                                                                                                              CIP

Contents

Introduction 3
The cost of quality, past and present; what has been offered to the apartment-consuming public and how has it been marketed.

Antecedents of American Apartments 10
The origins of apartments: ancient Roman; seventeenth- and eighteenth-century Scottish; an 1804 condominium conversion still extant in London.

Huckstering Hubert 17
Philip Hubert, grandfather of the co-op concept in New York; the Rembrandt, the Chelsea, 121 Madison Avenue, the Navarro.

Grand Gramercy 24
Dowager queen of co-op apartments at 34 Gramercy Park.

Residential Rustication 27
The Osborne at 205 West 57th Street.

Audacious Ansonia 33
Fashionably French flamboyance at Broadway and West 73rd Street.

Halfway Houses 38
Apartments aspiring to residential respectability: double-height studios, multifloor units, semiduplexes, interlocking units.

Dramatic des Artistes 43
Sumptuous studios for aesthetic affluence at One West 67th Street.

Gotham Gothic   52
   Theatricality and spaciousness at 44 West 77th Street.

Commodious Courtyards   56
   *An escape from the Manhattan street grid: the Dakota,
   Graham Court, the Apthorp, the Belnord, 1185 Park Avenue.*

Lexington Luxury   63
   *Affluent living adjoining Gramercy Park at One Lexington
   Avenue.*

Faux French   67
   The ersatz Beaux-Arts St. Urban at 285 Central Park West.

Parisian Prasada   72
   Spacious solidity at 50 Central Park West.

Hudson on the Hudson   77
   The Hendrik Hudson at 380 Riverside Drive.

Regal Riverside   83
   *Continental grandeur overlooking the river at 404 Riverside
   Drive.*

Eclectic Elegance   91
   Hard-fought survival and rebirth at 45 East 66th Street.

Resurrection Redux   94
   Alwyn Court is twice reborn at 180 West 58th Street.

Meandering Montana   98
   *Apartment appellations depict a wandering West, with a
   settlement at 375 Park Avenue, the third of four apartment
   houses named Montana.*

Holdout House 103
   *The last of its breed at 417 Park Avenue; how lower Park
   Avenue developed and then changed after World War II.*

Silent Sentinels   108
*Limestone reticence along Fifth Avenue: 907, 845, 834, 825 and
820 Fifth Avenue; Nixon and Rockefeller at 810 Fifth Avenue;
a 1910 Kansas view of New York apartments.*

Built to Suit   113
*Custom planning at 1107 Fifth Avenue; the 54-room Hutton
triplex.*

Multiple Mansions   117
*Stacked status behind the modest façade of 820 Park Avenue;
the spectacular triplex of A. J. Kobler.*

Magnificent Maisonette   124
*Proudly palatial privacy at 666 Park Avenue: a huge multi-
floored maisonette apartment that Imelda Marcos wanted.*

Penthouse Podium   130
*Rus in urbe atop 1010 Fifth Avenue: the lavish penthouse of
Fred F. French, and some architectural detective work.*

Bulky Beresford   135
*Classically triple-towered and terraced at 211 Central Park
West; Emery Roth as a self-made immigrant architect succeed-
ing in an alien world.*

Tuscan Tapestry   140
Texture and terra-cotta at 898 Park Avenue.

Ersatz English   145
*A vestigial memory of London at London Terrace on West 23rd
Street and Ninth Avenue; builder Henry Mandel versus
holdout Tillie Hart.*

Riverfront Refuge   151
*Exclusive enclave at 435 East 52nd Street; the great Christmas
tree battle, or, who owned the penthouse terrace?*

Depression Deco   157
*A practical response to an altered economy: the Century
Apartments at 25 Central Park West.*

Majestic Moderne 161
Twin-towered testament to zigzags and zoning: the Majestic Apartments at 115 Central Park West; Irwin Chanin's predictions.

Modified Mansion 165
Joseph Pulitzer's palace designed by McKim, Mead & White at 11 East 73rd Street becomes layered luxury lodgings.

Toney Tenement 170
Co-op conversion of Vanderbilt's visionary Shively Sanitary Tenements at East 77th Street and Cherokee Place.

Residential Recycling 174
Offices to apartments in lower Manhattan: the Potter Building facing City Hall, and Liberty Tower on Liberty Place.

Phantom Fashion 177
A grand cooperative apartment house at 960 Park Avenue . . . that never existed.

Shrinking Space 180
The evolving New York–apartment floor plan: the extremes, an 18-room full-floor suite at 903 Park Avenue, and a one-bedroom unit at the Century Apartments, 25 Central Park West.

Index 183

LUXURY
APARTMENT HOUSES
OF MANHATTAN

Figure 1. *The Stuyvesant, at 142 East 18th Street, shown in a view of 1934, was designed by Richard Morris Hunt and built by Rutherford Stuyvesant. It was filed with the New York City Department of Buildings in 1869, was completed during the summer of 1870 and was razed in 1957. It is often credited as having been the first apartment house in New York. (Charles von Urban, courtesy of the Museum of the City of New York.)*

Introduction

The cost of quality, past and present

APARTMENT LIVING IS ENDEMIC to New York, with cooperative or condominium ownership the dominant mode for luxury buildings. Not all expensive apartments can be considered to be in the "luxury" category, but those that are truly luxurious will most certainly carry a large price tag.

Traditionally, the three elements that create value in real estate have been location, location and location. Once that has been established, however, what else can be offered to justify a "luxury" price? A commercial building generates income, and the potential cash flow and tax benefits will help determine the price. But what creates value in residential real estate? Looking at the past might give us a clue to the present.

At some point prior to 1870, "French flats" were introduced to New York, either by Valentine Mott, Richard Morris Hunt, David Jardine, or by some unknown builder, depending on which reference you choose *(Figure 1)*. Such then-novel living units were distinguished from the earlier lower-class tenement houses in a number of ways. Each apartment had a parlor for entertaining and a separate dining room for eating; the kitchen was treated as merely a service space. Indoor plumbing was not shared with any other family, and there was generally a small room for a servant. These physical arrangements reflected the social customs of a moderately affluent family. Clearly, such apartments were different from tenements, and would appeal to a different market: the bourgeoisie.

To reach this market, developers recognized that they would have to make a clear distinction between the new French flats and the old tenements, particularly if the move toward apartment living was to be

more than a fad. Very few tenement houses of the nineteenth century had names, and those that did usually memorialized the female family members of their developers. There are the Sylvia at Columbus Avenue and West 76th Street, the Rose at Manhattan Avenue and West 109th Street and the Enid on West 96th Street.

As most of the lower-class accommodations bore only street addresses, what better way to give distinction to the new apartment buildings than with distinctive names? The variety of those names covered a wide range of marketing concepts. The earliest ones tended to reflect this country's strong English heritage: Albany, Berkeley, Berkshire, Blenheim, Carlyle, Chatsworth, Cornwall, Grosvenor, Hamilton, Westminster, Windemere, Windsor and the ultimate, Buckingham Palace (555 West 147th Street).

Before long, a Francophilia enveloped the city, with French names fighting their way to the forefront. There were such glitteringly Gallic examples as Bordeaux, Cherbourg, Grenoble, Lafayette, Paris, Rochambeau, Versailles and Beau Séjour. Scotland received its due with Dundonald, Dunsbro and later Duncraggan and Dunwell. Spain was represented by Barcelona, Cordova, El Casco, Granada, El Greco, Madrid, El Nido, Salamanca and Sevilla. Germany had Hohen-Au and Hohenzollern (in two versions), and Italy the Palermo, the Venice and the Roma.

Perhaps the most appropriate names were American. The native Americans were memorialized with the Waumbek, the Wanaque and the Waramaug, as well as the Iroquois, the Seminole, the Onondaga and the Cayuga. More widespread (and persistent over the

Figure 2. *The Wyoming in 1906, when it was the last word in luxury-apartment accommodations, providing 49 suites of 7 to 13 rooms. (Wurts Brothers, courtesy of the Museum of the City of New York.)*

years), however, was the use of state names for apartment houses.

Among early examples were the Idaho (version 1), a modest five-story building at 153 East 48th Street, now gone; the Idaho (version 2), a 12-story pile at 850 Seventh Avenue, since converted to office use; and the Arizona, eight stories of middle-class apartments at 508 West 114th Street, adjoining its mate, the Tennessee, at number 514. There was an Illinois at 511 West 113th Street, as well as two Indianas within a few blocks of each other, one at 117 West 79th Street and the other at 127 West 82nd Street. The stand-in for the state of Nevada was a free-standing seven-story brick block at Broadway and West 70th Street, designed in 1912 by Lafayette Goldstone and since

replaced with an anonymous eponymous modern tower, while Ohio could be found incongruously at 200 West 79th Street. The Oregon Apartments sat sedately at 162 West 54th Street, and Washington (as state and as general) has been commemorated by several apartment houses of that name in various places around town.

The Wyoming was built in 1906 as a grand 12-story apartment house with a weather-protected carriage driveway at Seventh Avenue and West 55th Street. The building is still there, although it has deteriorated badly, and the carriage drive has long since been converted to space for stores. No one remembers that it was once the proud Wyoming *(Figure 2)*.

The most famous "Western" apartment house is

probably the Dakota, at One West 72nd Street (*Figure 3*). The customary story of how it got its name is that developer Edward Clark was teased by his friends about the location of his new venture—so far away from civilization that it might just as well be in the Dakota territory. Architecture historian Christopher Gray has discovered that the true tale lies deeper than the popular assumption, and that Clark may have intended the name right from the beginning. More than eight months before construction began on the Dakota Apartments—in February 1880—Clark was quoted in a journal of the time as proposing that the emerging West Side should have appropriately Western street names. He suggested that Central Park West (then simply Eighth Avenue) ought to be called Montana Place, that Columbus Avenue should be Wyoming Place, that Amsterdam Avenue might logically become Arizona Place and that Idaho Place would be most suitable as a new name for West End Avenue.

Even with fancy names on their apartment-house projects, however, developers still had to breach a

Figure 3. *The Dakota, designed by Henry Janeway Hardenburgh and completed in 1884. The photograph is from 1928. (Wurts Brothers, courtesy of the Museum of the City of New York.)*

substantial wall of resistance. To counter this, they generally offered grandly expansive suites of rooms and a lavishness of finish and attention to detail far beyond what any tenement could present.

Typical of such an approach was the Osborne at West 57th Street and Seventh Avenue, completed in 1885 to designs of James Edward Ware. It was so lavish that ultimately it bankrupted its builder, Thomas Osborne. Built two blocks away at about the same time was the Central Park Apartments, designed by Hubert, Pirsson & Company. It too proved the undoing of its builder because of its massive cost.

Of the same vintage was the Dakota, which offered the obligatory high ceilings, large rooms, heavily lavish details and rich materials. Edward Clark handled its costs more effectively than other developers and considered the venture to be a success. His enticements to potential renters included a large wine cellar, extensive kitchens and a baronial dining hall for the private parties of the residents.

Following the successes of these early ventures, other developers entered the field. There were basically two distinct markets for the apartments built before World War I: There were the families who had lived in brownstones or town houses and who now wanted the convenience of an apartment; and there were the former tenement dwellers whose living standard had risen.

On the Upper West Side of Manhattan, many apartment houses were erected for former private-home dwellers. The builders attempted to show that living in them would have all the advantages of living in a private house as well as many amenities not available elsewhere. This meant water-filtration systems, central vacuum-cleaning machinery, central refrigeration plants (to eliminate the need for old-fashioned ice-boxes), built-in wall safes, and telephone switchboard services for both local and long-distance calls. Much was made of the ability to leave the city on holiday merely by locking one's front door instead of going through the elaborate ritual of closing up a house.

A famous cartoonist of the day parodied the efforts of the real-estate entrepreneurs by showing a drawing of a "modern" housewife in her new apartment kitchen, which is equipped with automatic delivery chutes from her suppliers of domestic provisions (*Figure 4*). Another cartoon by the same artist depicted a family sitting in its apartment home and enjoying the forerunners of radio and television: listening devices for lectures, concerts, theater and the opera; and automatic print-out machines serving up the daily newspapers for the adults and pictures to entertain the children (*Figure 5*).

Such lavishness was suitable for the upper classes, but there was also a cadre of buildings constructed for the expanding middle class. To keep costs at an affordable level for these people, builders developed their ventures in outlying areas where land was cheaper. There was a side advantage to this, however, since it offered grass, trees and open spaces to those who had previously lived in crowded sections of the city, far from parks or country air. Naturally, apartment layouts of this class were modest, with fewer and smaller rooms.

Builders were quick to recognize, however, that their renters would want to show their friends that they had risen in the world. A dining room separate from the kitchen was thus significant, and was included in one-bedroom apartments as well as in larger ones. Even if space was cramped, social imperatives dictated its inclusion, showing that dinner was now a ritual for the occupants. It also served as the real "living" room of the house, since the parlor was reserved for formal entertainment of visitors.

As apartment houses were developed, the sizes and proportions of rooms were considered more important than their relative configuration. The *enfilade* of European houses was rejected in favor of the privacy separate hallways afforded. Beyond that, however, there was little to recommend the early plans. There were few grand entrance halls or reception spaces, and rooms were strung out along narrow corridors. Bathrooms were often remote from bedrooms, and kitchens were widely separated from dining rooms.

But, as the twentieth century proceeded, so did the thoughtfulness of apartment layouts. Advertisements featured descriptions of the functional arrangements of the rooms, and floor plans were printed and widely distributed to lure the potential renter or purchaser. Effective space was the inducement. By the early 1920s, layouts offered pleasing spatial experiences.

Room sizes were reduced, however, and the standard architectural detailing and ornamentation were simplified. This reflected changing tastes in decorating. The overscaled and overstuffed furniture of the nineteenth century and its attendant clutter had given way to more modestly scaled furnishings. The greater range of acceptable decorating styles meant that a plainer architectural background would be less inhibiting for a creative housewife.

As the 1920s rolled into the 1930s, the Depression meant that reducing and simplifying space was as economically important to builders as it was to apartment dwellers. Minimal housing budgets forced families into smaller and smaller quarters. Designers of apartment houses used their imaginations to devise architectural features such as the ubiquitous sunken living room (down two or three steps from the foyer) and the dining "gallery," which might offer visual compensation and the illusion of greater space.

The march of time in the half-century since then has brought with it a similarly relentless march

Figure 4. *"In the Kitchen," by Frederick Burr Opper, 1883.*

Figure 5. *"In the Parlor," by Frederick Burr Opper, 1883.*

downward in the sizes of apartments and their component rooms. First to go was the so-called formal dining room, justified by the assumption that "modern" living was more informal, and that an alcove off the living room would suffice for an eating area. Even this has more recently been reduced still further to a corner of the living room itself, with the function accommodated merely by the identification "dining area" on the rental and sales plans.

Next were the bedrooms. Families of today are smaller than those of preceding generations, and three-bedroom apartments have become an extreme rarity, with four-bedroom units almost completely unheard-of. Even the two-bedroom apartment is

rapidly being transmogrified into a one-bedroom with a "convertible" dining bay adjacent to the living room. One-bedroom apartments have become as small in total area as the studios of only a few years ago, and what purport to be luxury studios in the most recent advertisements would barely qualify as the transient or student accommodations of the recent past.

During the 1930s, the reduction in space was justified and accompanied by a comparable reduction in cost. Today, however, the opposite is true. Apartment sizes are plummeting while prices skyrocket. Cramped one-room "efficiency" apartments in secondary locations carry price tags of $200,000 and more, and decent-sized one-bedroom apartments in the most desirable neighborhoods *begin* at half a million dollars.

In the nineteenth century, the value in an apartment suite was created first by the ability to maintain a suitable city residence without the inconvenience of a private house. The number of servants needed to run a household was sharply reduced, privacy was increased and added amenities were available.

As the concept of apartment living developed and matured, rooms became larger and apartments more spacious. Reception areas and circulation spaces were made more gracious and were complemented by more elegant materials and architectural detailing. Functional improvements were made, and amenities added that made apartment living easier and more refined.

Today, with apartment living virtually the only show in town, and with multimillion-dollar apartments regularly advertised, the question still stands: What is it that creates the value, and what is it that justifies the prices?

It is a cliché to say that the world has changed, but it is particularly apt when trying to understand why the apartments being offered today differ so significantly from those of the past. The most obvious change is in the question of space. While there are buildings with floor plans comparable to those of earlier years, these are the exceptions, and their prices *are* exceptional. For the more "normal" offerings, the room sizes and configurations now demand far more clever furniture planning and decorative schemes if effective use is to be made of the available square footage.

The ostensibly luxurious materials found in the finishing of the newer apartments are but pale reflections of long ago: "parquet" floors consist of thin pieces of prefinished wood of secondary grade carelessly glued to an inadequately leveled concrete slab. "Marble" bathrooms merely substitute thin marble tiles for the more conventional glazed ceramic ones. And "plaster" walls are half-inch-thick sheets of paper-wrapped gypsum wallboard, originally devised for the rapid construction of offices and of subsidized housing for those at the lowest levels of society.

The idea of what constitutes the "right" neighborhood is also different. Super-expensive apartment houses are being erected in out-of-the-way locales that may be inconveniently situated or may be surrounded by tenement houses or secondary commercial structures.

And the elevator men, doormen, hall attendants and armies of backstairs service personnel available at all hours are no more, or at least are not as they used to be.

The claim that developers are too greedy is an oversimplification. Those who invest in real estate have always done so in the hope of making a profit, and people today still want to make money from their efforts.

The biggest problem is that costs everywhere have risen. The price of the land under new buildings is very high, which means that sites in secondary, less expensive, locations are used. The price for materials—steel, concrete, brick—is also significant. And finish materials are more expensive, with the finest ones no longer practical for use in speculative ventures.

In addition, labor costs have risen dramatically. This is not really surprising, since the expectations of workers are much greater now. High-school graduates, and even college-degreed workers are not unusual on construction projects, and this education, coupled with the blandishments of mass advertising and the aggressiveness of union negotiating teams, has yielded much higher wage rates and benefit packages than existed when the earlier "grand old" apartment houses were being built.

All this requires a steady cash-flow from the developer, which can come only from borrowed funds. And with interest rates usually high, and construction times longer because of building complexities and union-mandated artificial limitations on worker productivity, there is a larger money-cost factor involved.

These elements combine to create a smaller individual apartment unit that costs more to purchase and more to maintain. But there is another aspect that has had a very strong impact on builders: life-style.

It has been said that it is the sizzle which is being marketed rather than the steak, and perhaps that is true. But the advertising reflects what is being offered, which in turn reflects what is sought by the targeted market. One market component that has not changed for decades is this: people seeking adequate space in pleasant, safe surroundings. The offerings to those consumers are not as large or as luxurious as they used to be for the financial reasons already delineated, but within the economic realities, developers *are* producing decent and adequate housing. Much of it is on the West Side, and it is advertised in terms of traditional value-for-money.

There is a newer component, however, which puts more stress on the "life-style," and it is toward that target that the more flamboyant offerings are aimed.

This group tends to be younger and is interested in physical fitness, in looking good, in having a good time, in being successful (or at least in creating an image of success) and in socializing more in restaurants and clubs than at home. Its acquisitions are generally more compact: compact-disc stereo systems and video recorders rather than space-consuming sculptures, grand pianos or large and impressive pieces of furniture.

For this market, the apartment houses offer much

less space. But they compensate for this in ways that meet a definite need. Much of this is emotional, but the means to reach it are very real.

The Rio, at East 65th Street and Second Avenue, for instance, used this approach in its sales brochure:

> Sensual. Exhilarating. Exciting. That's Brazil's electrifying Rio. And that's the inspiration for Manhattan's Rio. This sleek and glamorous 40-story residential tower brings a new kind of excitement to living in Manhattan. Here's a home to be pampered in. To entertain and to party in. To relax, work out and be yourself in. And, if you choose, to just hide away in.

Clearly, the Rio is offering a life-style, and one that is the goal of a significant segment of New York's young, hard-pushing, high-achievers. "Sleek and glamorous" are the words used by the copywriter to describe the building, and those same adjectives depict what the Rio's potential buyers aspire to be. In traditional terms this *is* sizzle and not steak, but it is sizzle that is being sought, and it is sizzle that sells.

But who is to say that the sizzle is inherently less important than the steak? Quoting again, this time from the sales brochure for Memphis Uptown, an anorectic tower overlooking the access ramp to the 59th Street Bridge:

> Because this is New York and these are the 1980s, what we are experiencing is the growth of a new attitude toward objects around us and the environments we live in: we are expecting them to not merely look good but to energize and amuse us. This is something radically different from what came before. We have finally come around to the daring idea that, in addition to being correctly proportioned or related to function or timelessness, design is supposed to be alive. Not placed on a pedestal but lived in and enjoyed. Not analyzed or appraised but appreciated in the relaxed environments of our homes.

Is this merely the huckster's hype, the excuse offered for giving less and charging more? Or is it perhaps a reflection of a more basic change in our values?

At any instant of historical time there is no one "way of life" that completely reflects a particular society. Sociologists and historians categorize and pigeonhole, but real humans are more elusive. A New Yorker is supposed to be very different from a Londoner or a Roman, yet, on an individual basis, there is a complex crossing over and interweaving of personalities and life-styles. And so it is with those seeking apartment accommodations. Ultimately, there is no single approach that is "right," and no single buyer who is "typical."

The then-outlandish Dorilton at West 71st Street and Broadway was scorned by tradition-minded apartment seekers at the beginning of this century, just as their counterparts today scorn so much new construction and long for the good old days. Plus ça change . . .

Some buildings offer plain vanilla space and few amenities beyond a laundry room. Others tout their skyline views, their health clubs and their multilingual concierges. And others market themselves like perfume, offering an image of what their product represents rather than what it actually is. Is one any better than the next as a more realistic value?

In the end, they are all "right." Each caters to a different need, to a different customer, to a different segment of the market. Each justifies itself on its own terms and each fills a niche. Only occasionally does one fail totally. The entertainer Liberace was the sole buyer in an apartment house on East 55th Street that failed (and was later reborn as a hotel). But for most ventures, the developer produces a concept (or he hires a marketing consultant to create one) and then constructs a building to fulfill it. His copywriters and graphic artists prepare advertising brochures. He presents his offerings to the public. And then, rapidly or slowly, he sells the units and fills up his building.

Each developer is both a unique individual and a product of his time, and each new apartment house reflects this. There are those who will always prefer the old and the traditional, and those who will always seek the newest and the most different. And it is the glory of New York that there is ample room for both.

Antecedents of American Apartments

The origin of apartments

IT HAS BEEN SAID that a New Yorker discovered America, that a New Yorker invented gunpowder and that New York is the center of civilization. Whether or not these "facts" be true is perhaps subject to debate, but it is incontrovertible that New York did not spawn the first apartment house. Indeed, it was not even home to the first one under cooperative or condominium ownership. To understand the multiple-dwellings found in all major cities in America, we need to look first at their origins, which go back a lot farther than might be expected. Of particular interest is a prime early-nineteenth-century example still existing in London, which serves as a model that has been emulated in New York.

Tenement apartments for the lower classes were known in ancient Rome, with primitive *insulæ* reaching as high as six stories. Cheaply built, they frequently collapsed, an event depicted to vivid effect in the movie *Fellini's Satyricon*.

Apartment living for middle-class families was a very early feature of Scottish urban life. Indeed, the British term for apartment—flat—is merely a relatively recent corruption of the Scottish *flæt,* a word used as early as the twelfth century to mean an independent suite of rooms.

There were blocks of flats, or apartment houses, in Edinburgh by the middle of the 1400s. Although none still exists, a seven-story apartment house in Waldrop's

Court, Edinburgh, was erected in the seventeenth century, and appears to be the oldest to have survived into modern times in approximately its original form *(Figure 6)*. The apartments were designed one to a floor, each with sitting rooms, bedrooms, quarters for servants, a kitchen and tiny windowed "closets" (originally without plumbing, of course). Legal decisions of the period indicate that individual fee ownership of Edinburgh's apartments by their residents was normal, thus qualifying them as an early form of condominium.

Speculative building of apartment houses in Scotland was widespread, and in 1696 a law restricted such buildings to no more than five stories, and specified the minimum thickness of the walls at each story. By the late eighteenth century, fine apartment houses for the wealthy were normal in Edinburgh, with Sir Walter Scott living in a particularly elegant Classically fronted one in Castle Street from 1798 to 1826 *(Figure 7)*.

London was slow to adopt flat-living as the norm for families, but it had an ancient tradition since the Middle Ages of stacked chambers for bachelors. The very term "chambers" is still used for the offices of English lawyers, perpetuating the memory that they once lived there, sleeping behind the store, as it were.

That tradition of acceptability for moneyed males to live in separate sets of rooms within a single building resulted in the antecedent of the luxury co-

Opposite: Figure 6. *A middle-class apartment house from the 1600s in Waldrop's Court, Edinburgh, Scotland, photographed in 1904. Even today there is no elevator. (Sydney Perks.)*

Figure 7. *A 1904* view of the eighteenth-century apartment house in Edinburgh, Scotland, occupied for 28 years by Sir Walter Scott. *(Sydney Perks.)*

ops and condominiums of New York City, and the oldest such apartment house is still operating exactly as it did when it was first created in 1804.

Albany, in London's Piccadilly, offers apartments (called "sets of chambers") to those with sufficient money and social connections to pass the scrutiny of its Board of Trustees, which administers its affairs in much the same way a co-op or condominium board of directors does in America.

The physical origins of Albany date to 1771, when Baron Melbourne of Kilmore bought property in Piccadilly for £16,500. It was his wife, however, who directed the design and construction of a grand mansion on the site.

The new house took four years to complete, with Lady Melbourne directing the entire affair. Lord Melbourne merely groused about the cost and paid the bills, which totaled an astounding £50,000 *(Figure 8)*.

Excessive expenditures to support the extravagant living style of Lord and Lady Melbourne precipitated the acquisition of their house in 1791 by Frederick, the Duke of York and Albany. This younger son of King George III was also addicted to high living, and in 1802 he too was forced to sell the house, at a loss of almost £30,000 from its original cost.

The buyer was Alexander Copland, a real-estate developer, who hired the architect Henry Holland to convert the mansion to more "modern" uses.

Figure 8. *An illustration of ca. 1775 shows the house in Piccadilly as built by Lord and Lady Melbourne.* (Carlton House Magazine.)

Holland began by replacing the porter's lodge and gate on Piccadilly with a pair of shops surmounted with apartments, and reduced the size of the forecourt with additional apartment construction *(Figures 9 & 10)*. He then subdivided the grand house of Lady Melbourne's conception into a grouping of apartments *(Figure 11)*.

The exceptionally deep garden out back was sacrificed to a pair of long buildings, which contained apartments opening off individual stairhalls. Access to these was gained via a covered walkway. Perhaps because of its great length, this open corridor has always been known as the Rope Walk *(Figure 12)*. The conversion and new construction work were completed in 1804.

There are a total of 70 apartments in Albany. Those converted from the rooms of the original mansion are, of course, each unique. The purpose-built ones in the garden buildings each originally comprised an anteroom, a large living room, a large bedroom, a small dressing room and a bathroom, all on one floor, plus a kitchen in the basement and a servant's room on the top floor. The main floors of the apartments were stacked three high, with each stairwell serving six apartments.

Over the years, many alterations have been made, with these room groupings expanded or contracted as the personal needs of their residents dictated. Because all the rooms of any one apartment are not necessarily contiguous, they are called "sets" of chambers rather than flats.

What made Albany especially distinctive and unusual then, and continues to do so today, is the form of ownership and management. Sets of rooms can be owned outright in fee simple, as a New York condominium unit would be. They can also be owned in fee farm, in which an annual rent is due a previous owner in perpetuity, or they can be leased from an owner who may be absent or may be living in alternative rooms within Albany.

Ownership of the common elements of Albany vests in its Board of Trustees, as does complete control over the operation of the complex. Each leaseholder of an apartment and each proprietor (as owners of these sets of rooms are known) must sign a Deed of Covenant to abide by the rules and regulations set forth by the Board of Trustees before he (or she, since the early 1880s) is permitted to purchase or lease rooms in Albany.

Although Albany is located in the center of London, and opens onto bustling Piccadilly, it has been maintained from its inception as a place of refuge for its residents. The novelist Marmion Savage "fictionally" described Albany, perhaps not without accuracy, as

Opposite, top: Figure 9. *The original entrance to Melbourne House from Piccadilly, as depicted ca. 1775. On the left is the protective forecourt wall of Burlington House. (Courtesy of the Soane Museum.)* Opposite, bottom: Figure 10. *The new entrance from Piccadilly as designed by Henry Holland, in a view of 1804. The wall of Burlington House can still be seen to the left, although it was later removed when the present front building was erected. The shop-fronted buildings of Holland were also later replaced. (Courtesy of Sheila Birkenhead.)* Above: Figure 11. *The mansion house of Albany, as it appeared in 1904 having served for a century as a multiple dwelling. (Sydney Perks.)*

the haunt of bachelors, or of married men who try to lead bachelors' lives; the dread of suspicious wives, the retreat of superannuated fops, the hospital for incurable oddities, a cluster of solitudes for social hermits, the home of homeless gentlemen, the diner-out and the diner-in, the place for the fashionably thrifty, the luxuriously lonely, and the modishly morose, the votaries of melancholy, and lovers of mutton-chops.

While Mr. Savage may have been taking a bit of artistic license with his specific descriptions, Albany has indeed been rather strangely removed from the world around it. The "fierce porters" who guarded its gates in the nineteenth century have been replaced by modern computer-encoded plastic entry cards, but the privacy being protected has remained constant.

It was the ability to retreat from worldly pressures within the walls of Albany that attracted such politicians as Prime Minister William Gladstone and the

lesser luminary Edward Heath, the pioneer photographer William Henry Fox Talbot, the musician Sir Thomas Beecham, and writers (who probably cherished the privacy most of all) Graham Greene, Aldous Huxley, J. B. Priestley, Thomas Babington Macaulay and the most famous of all, Lord Byron. Most of the current residents of Albany continue the tradition of seeking anonymity, and only the decorator David Hicks and the American Fleur Cowles are known to advertise openly that they live there.

Quite a number of fictional characters have "openly" dwelled in sets at Albany, however. Fascination Fledgeby was a "resident" according to Charles Dickens, writing in *Our Mutual Friend.* Lord Lufton of Sir Anthony Trollope's *Framley Parsonage* lived there, as did Ernest of Oscar Wilde's *The Importance of Being Earnest.* In more modern times, Terence Rattigan's *While the Sun Shines* was set in Albany.

But even the fictional residents and visitors to

Albany recognized the special character of the place. In *Sinister Street,* Compton Mackenzie wrote:

> He enjoyed the intense silence that brooded outside the heavily curtained windows. Here in Albany, Michael was immeasurably aware of the life of London that was surging such a little distance away; but in this modish cloister he felt that the life he was aware of could never be dated, as if indeed he were to emerge into Piccadilly and behold suddenly crinolines or even powdered wigs they would not greatly surprise him.

The "intense silence" of which Mackenzie wrote in 1914 was replaced a few years ago by pneumatic drills and intense construction activity in Sackville Street, directly to the east of Albany. The Board of Trustees then found themselves with problems similar to those encountered increasingly by urban residents all over the world: intrusions and security. The alterations to the Sackville Street buildings made security breaches a greater worry, and it was suggested to apartment owners that bars be installed to secure vulnerable windows. The realities of modern living had come to plague even the most prestigious of accommodations in London.

The adjustments required by urban ills notwithstanding, Albany remains a paradigm of luxurious apartment living and the prototype for numerous buildings in New York City.

Figure 12. *The Rope Walk leading to the purpose-built apartments of Albany, 1904. (Sydney Perks.)*

Huckstering Hubert

Grandfather of the co-op concept in New York

"REMBRANDT REDUX" MIGHT WELL be an appropriate name for the office building recently erected to the west of the holdout Russian Tea Room, since that structure sits on the site of what Christopher Gray has determined was the first cooperative development in New York City—the eight-story Rembrandt at 152 West 57th Street *(Figure 13)*.

Erected in 1881 to the designs of the French-born architect Philip Gengembre Hubert, the Rembrandt was the prototype of a bevy of other cooperative apartment ventures brought to fruition over the ensuing years. Of these, the Gramercy, at 34 Gramercy Park, is the oldest one still extant and operating as a co-op.

Hubert liked the idea of an apartment house owned by a group of investors, each of whom would have a proprietary lease to an apartment in the building. He felt that its flexibility made it an appropriate alternative to owning a brownstone row house or other private dwelling. There were many benefits: more expansive and better arrangements for entertaining, increased light and air, views, greater security and ease of closing an apartment for a holiday and more potential privacy and anonymity.

But perhaps most attractive to Hubert's business sense were the benefits of scale inherent in the joining together of many families to provide for their housing needs. With a centralized heating plant, coordinated garbage disposal, package-delivery provisions and even joint cooking and dining facilities, the total cost of keeping house could be significantly reduced.

At the same time, Hubert recognized that the class of New Yorkers to whom he intended to market his new "cooperative" apartments would be at least as concerned with appearances as with price, so he sought in his planning to provide facilities that would be as socially acceptable as they would be fiscally sound.

Playing on his adopted English language for all it was worth, Hubert dubbed his ventures "Hubert Home Clubs," capitalizing on both the aristocratic pretensions and snob appeal of the word "club," and at the same time emphasizing that his offerings were permanent "homes," rather than mere hotellike accommodations or lowly tenement flats such as might be occupied by the working classes. In his own way, Philip G. Hubert was as much a huckster of "life-style" as are the developer marketers of today's latest superslick offerings. The purveyors of the more recent cellular condominiums present their offerings much as Hubert did: as rungs on a social ladder.

The Chelsea, erected in 1883, was one of the original buildings designed and marketed by the architect and his firm, Hubert, Pirsson & Company *(Figure 14)*. The West 23rd Street landmark opened as a co-op, but was later converted to a hotel, and is distinctive for its lacy cast-iron balconies *(Figure 15)* and its renowned tenants (who included Dylan Thomas and Sid Vicious, among others). The structure underwent extensive exterior renovations a few years ago, the direct result of a near-fatal accident when the balcony fronting on the apartment of resident Alphæus Cole (who died some time after at the age of 112) suddenly broke loose and crashed down, shattering on the pavement below.

Number 121 Madison Avenue was more representa-

Figure 13. *The Rembrandt, 152 West 57th Street, the first cooperative apartment house in New York, ca. 1905. (Courtesy of The New-York Historical Society.)*

Figure 14. *The Chelsea, at 222 West 23rd Street, ca. 1908, shortly after its conversion from a cooperative apartment house to a hotel.*
(J. P. Day, courtesy of The New-York Historical Society.)

Figure 15. *The façade of The Chelsea, showing its lacelike floral cast-iron balcony railings, 1936. (Berenice Abbott, courtesy of the Museum of the City of New York.)*

tive of Hubert's Home Clubs than the Chelsea, but it has suffered greatly. As originally erected in 1883, it consisted of five grandly spacious duplex apartments for each two floors of the building. The entertaining rooms were on the lower levels, with much greater ceiling heights than the bedrooms, which were on the upper levels. The largest of the apartments had five entertaining rooms opening *en suite* via sliding mahogany and etched-glass doors: reception room, library, drawing room, parlor and dining room.

After World War I, the neighborhood—the corner of Madison Avenue and East 30th Street—declined rapidly. The Great Depression gave the building the *coup de grâce,* with the structure's brutal and insensitive alteration in 1940 into a conventional rental

building with tiny two- and three-room apartments.

While the desecration of the apartment interiors are mercifully hidden from passersby, the rape of its façade is not. At the top of the building additional stories were inartistically grafted on, the cornice and the decorative balconies were lobotomized, virtually all the ornamentation was stripped away and the ground floor so tastelessly altered as to defy description. All that is left to hint at what the building once was is the color of the brick, the alternating high and low floor-to-floor heights, and a single belt course of decorative pressed ornamental brick just above the third floor.

Perhaps the grandest project Philip Hubert ever conceived was ill-starred even before it opened.

Figure 16. *The Central Park Apartments, more commonly known as The Navarro, ca. 1890. (Courtesy of The New-York Historical Society.)*

Officially called the Central Park Apartments, this eight-building complex was often called the Spanish Flats because of the names of its individual units: Madrid, Cordova, Granada, Valencia, Lisbon, Barcelona, Saragossa and Tolosa. More commonly, however, its was known as the Navarro, after its original builder, one José (or Juan) de Navarro *(Figures 16 & 17).*

An original prospectus for the venture called for completion of the entire project about October 1883, and invited purchasers to pay in ten installments the total purchase prices for corner apartments of $20,000 and for inside apartments of $15,000. There were special double-sized units on the upper floors, and these of course carried premium prices. Each of the eight buildings was to be structured as an individual

cooperative corporation, or "Home Club," with equal access to the common elements of the development which by their nature were to be shared by all the buildings.

To keep the necessary cash investments for each apartment owner reduced, the buildings would be erected on leased land. But each corporation would have the right at any time to purchase the land under its building at prices ranging from $166,667 for the least desirable buildings to $250,000 for the ones fronting Seventh Avenue. The leased-land concept was to be the downfall of the entire venture.

The project encompassed a huge plot running from West 58th to West 59th Streets at Seventh Avenue. There was a private driveway that sloped down to the

Figure 17. *The Navarro, or Spanish Flats, as viewed from Central Park, directly to the north, ca. 1910. (Courtesy of The New-York Historical Society.)*

basement level at the center of the block, allowing tradesmen to bring their delivery wagons and carts directly into an underground street that served the eight buildings. This off-street delivery concept, which was also used for the decorous removal of the ashes and garbage, was employed in a reduced version at the Belnord Apartments of 1908, but would not be repeated at this scale until Rockefeller Center was built in the 1930s.

The sales offering touted the advantages of living within the development, noting that each building would be "composed of people socially suited to each other and intending to make the house not a temporary stopping place but a home." It promoted the idea of cooperative ownership by saying, "The Home Club System is not a new thing; it is simply an improvement on the European plan of joint ownership. In Scotland and Continental Europe the custom of owning a floor has existed for centuries, and is to this day a favorite way of owning a home in many parts of Europe."

Brownstone living was compared to living in a comparable amount of space in a co-op. Notice was made of the ability to throw together the reception rooms of the home for large-scale entertaining, a possibility not conveniently available in a brownstone, in which the "public" rooms might be separated on two or even three floors.

The special amenities of the buildings were to be ample: Entirely fireproof, they would contain stairs of iron and marble, steam heat and boiling water throughout, separate passenger and freight elevators and an artesian well supplying water to the buildings independent of the city's system.

All this was at projected annual costs that would be equivalent to a 17 percent return on the capital invested in the price of each individual apartment. But it was not to be. Hubert had retained ownership of the land on which the Spanish Flats were being erected. At the time construction costs began seriously exceeding the estimates and the available cash flow, he had not transferred ownership to the individual cooperative corporations. Mortgage holder J. Jennings McComb foreclosed and completed the development as a complex of rental buildings.

The cost of the entire project was $4 million, which by a curious coincidence was the price paid by the New York Athletic Club for one half of the property in 1925 as a site for its new home.

The Navarro was a grand and innovative scheme for a hitherto unknown way of living luxuriously in Manhattan. It was designed by an architect whose work remains in bits and pieces, but whose vision in promoting cooperative apartment houses is barely known and is certainly underappreciated. Philip G. Hubert died in 1912 at the age of 81. And what might have been his greatest memorial, the Navarro, was demolished only 15 years later.

Grand Gramercy

Dowager queen of co-op apartments at
34 Gramercy Park

IT WAS NOT THE first of its breed, but the Gramercy is the oldest one to have survived.

Two years after the Rembrandt was built on West 57th Street by Philip Hubert, another apartment house, similar in concept, opened more than two miles away, at 34 Gramercy Park and East 20th Street. Built on the site of the Gramercy Park House (a hotel; *Figure 18*), it had originally been planned as the Gramercy Family Hotel by developers James Campbell and John Duncan Phyfe, but during the early stages of its construction the pair sold their interest in the property and relocated operations to West 59th Street and Grand Army Plaza, where they erected the first Plaza Hotel. (It never opened, and remained vacant for several years until the mortgage holder foreclosed on the property and retained the architectural firm of McKim, Mead & White to alter the building significantly.)

The purchaser of the partially completed Gramercy Park project was a group of investors under the guidance of Judge William H. Arnoux. The group, which included William Duncan Phyfe, hotel entrepreneur Charles Gerlach and Haley Fiske (later president of the Metropolitan Life Insurance Company), was incorporated in March 1883. The group immediately altered the project's plans, turning the hotel into an apartment house by the time it opened in October 1883 *(Figure 19)*.

The Gramercy was designed by George W. Da Cunha, about whom almost nothing is known. At the time of his commission his offices were at 111 Broadway—the original Trinity Building. His son, who joined the practice in 1886, was elected a Fellow of the American Institute of Architects and died in 1894, but Da Cunha himself just seems to disappear after 1892.

For Judge Arnoux's group, Da Cunha designed a nine-story structure comprising 27 apartments, with bachelor and studio accommodations and servants' quarters under the roof. Although other cooperative ventures in the city generally featured duplex suites that approximated the feel of row houses, the Gramercy offered only simplex apartments, all on one level.

The three apartments on each floor contained seven, nine and 11 rooms apiece, yet each included only a single bathroom—even for the largest unit, which had five bedrooms. The custom of the time dictated that a man would be shaved each morning at his barber's and that far fewer showers were taken than today. A woman would spend more time at her vanity table in her boudoir covering her body with scents and creams than she might spend in her bath. For these reasons, multiple bathrooms were not considered particularly important a century ago.

Similarly of only passing concern was the arrange-

ment of the rooms, whose decorations were given more attention than room interrelationships. Thus in the eastern apartment on each floor a long and twisted entrance corridor leads to the dining room, through which one must walk to gain access to the rest of the flat. To get from one end of the northern apartment's inner hallway to the other, no fewer than six turns must be negotiated. And in each of the suites, the library (or everyday living room) must be crossed to get to the parlor (traditionally used only for entertaining visitors). Wardrobe units were built into the corners of some of the bedrooms, but no conventional closets were provided. There was a steam-heating system for the building, but fireplaces were constructed in all but the smallest rooms. Lighting was by gas, since the lines of the New York Edison Company did not reach far enough north to provide electricity. Any relation to apartment layouts and conveniences as we know them today was purely coincidental.

The fitments of the building—in mahogany, brass, mosaic tiles and stained glass—were richly provided, however, and included three silent-running elevators (two for goods and one for passengers). Powered by water pressure, each car is controlled by a cable running the full height of the building. The operator pulls on the cable to open or close the valves to the water tanks, enabling the car to go up or down. Installed by Otis Brothers & Company, these are the oldest such elevators extant that still operate as originally designed.

Another distinction of the Gramercy was the restaurant of Louis Sherry, who had an enviable reputation for producing lavish dinners and dramatic parties. Sherry's establishment was placed on the eighth floor, with only bachelor and servant rooms above, to reduce the disturbance of kitchen smells. It would be, said the lease, "a first class Restaurant equal in style and quality to Delmonicos." Meals could be taken in the dining room, or be sent to any apartment in the building (using Sherry's platters or the tenant's). For all the care and effort provided by Sherry, however, the venture did not prove a success, and the restaurant closed in less than a year.

Nineteen of the original 27 apartments were sold by Charles Gerlach as agent for the incorporated investors to tenant-owners at prices ranging from $10,800 for a seven-room suite overlooking the old Third Avenue Elevated Railway, and $19,200 for a nine-room one

with a view of Gramercy Park, to $20,720 for an 11-room apartment facing south. One special apartment was sold for $31,680 according to a real-estate journal of the period.

A marketing ploy curious by today's standards was the pricing structure. Each line of apartments had a single price per suite, regardless of how high up in the building it was located. In the days of walk-ups (and also among the original apartment houses of Europe), the flats on the upper floors were considered less desirable than the ones closer to the street. To avoid economic and social stratification within the building, Gerlach priced the apartments irrespective of floor level, extending this principle to the suites that were rented out as well.

If the name of the religious holiday Maundy Thursday has a curious ring to it, so does Thursby's Fridays. Among the original stockholder-tenants of the Gramercy were Max Strakosch, a noted impresario, and singer Emma Thursby, who was managed by Strakosch's brother, Maurice.

Purchasing her apartment months before the building was completed, Thursby was among the first to move into it in 1883; she stayed there until 1931, when death's eviction notice came at age 84. Emma Thursby concertized extensively in America and Europe and amassed a huge following. As her voice gradually lost its power, however, she curtailed her public concerts and devoted herself more to teaching her singing students, among whom was the renowned Geraldine Farrar. At the same time, she increased her socializing, and inaugurated weekly salons dubbed Thursby's Fridays. Each week a guest of honor received with her, among them Enrico Caruso, Edwin Markham, Nellie Melba, the Duc de Richelieu, Isadora Duncan and Rabindranath Tagore.

Thursby shared her home with her mother, two sisters and her two brothers. There were no servants' rooms within any of the apartments in the Gramercy, so the only other creature living within the flat was the mynah bird that had been presented to Thursby at one of her concerts in Germany. The bird talked in five languages and was popular with the children who played in Gramercy Park. He even traveled with Thursby on a tour to the Pacific Coast in 1892. When the bird died in 1899, his obituary appeared in the newspapers and the Thursby family received many letters of condolence.

Residential Rustication

The Osborne at 205 West 57th Street

IN NEW YORK CITY, almost anything that reaches the century mark is looked upon with awe. Considering the propensity of real-estate development to require the destruction of the old to make room for the new, it is rare indeed when an apartment house reaches its hundredth birthday. There are the Dakota and the Gramercy. And there is the venerable and much-loved Osborne *(Figure 20)*.

The Osborne's bulky presence diagonally opposite Carnegie Hall at West 57th Street and Seventh Avenue has always been familiar to concertgoers, since the apartment house is six years older than the hall. The musical connection has been augmented by an artistic one as well: the Art Students League building is nearby. That structure, adjoining on West 57th Street, was designed by Henry Janeway Hardenbergh (architect also of the Dakota) and erected the year after Carnegie Hall. Originally known as the American Fine Arts Society, it housed the Architectural League, the Society of American Artists and the Art Students League.

With the artists and architects next door and the musicians across the street, there has long been an idea that the Osborne was built—and is a haven—for artists and/or artistic types. Nonetheless, the tenant lists, at least up to the time of the Second World War, included lawyers, doctors, merchants and corporate executives—but no musicians, writers or artists, and only two architects.

Essentially, the Osborne was built for a decidedly upper-middle-class market. Physical evidence for this lies in the apartment sizes and layouts, in the decorative interior features and, perhaps most important, in the design of the exterior façade.

As originally designed by architect James Edward Ware (1846–1918), the Osborne occupied a site 150 feet wide on West 57th Street and 100 feet deep along Seventh Avenue. To the north on the avenue was the Central Park Livery Stables, with more stables and a riding academy on the next block. Across West 57th Street was the Grenoble Hotel (whose memory is preserved in the name of a present-day grocery store on the Osborne's ground floor), while adjoining to the west was a small brick house with a little wood building at the rear of its backyard. Although the site of Carnegie Hall was still a huge vacant lot, the residential nature of the neighborhood had already been established with the erection of the Rembrandt apartments on West 57th Street in 1881, and then two years later with the construction a block north of the eight-building Spanish Flats. Although commercial buildings abounded in the nearby blocks, the proximity of Central Park justified the use of some of the remaining vacant lots for the still relatively new-fangled French flats.

Apartment living had been introduced about 1870, with Philip G. Hubert later pioneering the concept of cooperatives. Most developers, however, confined themselves to rental buildings, and encouraged the signing of leases by the lavishness of the accommodations. Perhaps never in the history of apartment construction was so much bronze, marble and exotic wood used for multiple dwellings. The Saint Catherine, for example, was designed by architect Hugo Kafka and entirely filled a 47-by-100-foot lot with a single apartment on each floor. The entrance lobby to the building had woodwork of amaranth, windows of opaline glass, lighting fixtures of cut glass, sculptured

Figure 20. *The Osborne, as it looked originally, ca. 1886, when it still had its entrance porch, moat and balustrades, and before the top floor was extended along the Seventh Avenue side of the building. (Courtesy of The New-York Historical Society.)*

bronze work and decorative stained glass. Other developers imported tessera mosaic flooring from Italy, unusual woods from Central Europe and carved stone and terra-cotta from Germany, France and England. In the struggle to rent his buildings, each builder attempted to outdo the others in the luxury of his offerings.

Into this highly competitive environment ventured stone contractor Thomas Osborne. Together with his architect, James Ware, Osborne devised a marketing approach and a design that reflected it. Rejecting the complexities and expense of duplexes, Osborne and Ware planned an arrangement of four essentially similar apartments on each floor, served by two separate elevator/stair halls that were connected at the ground floor by an entrance lobby. There were to be 40 suites, some of which were provided with intermediate mezzanine levels at the back for additional bedrooms and servants' quarters. The fitments of each apartment were grand and lavish by our standards, but were quite expected then: 14-foot ceiling heights, mahogany woodwork, oak floors with elaborate parquetwork designs, bronze hardware, stained glass and drawn plaster moldings.

In 1876, the builders Duggin and Crossman had erected an apartment house on Fifth Avenue north of 52nd Street and named it the Osborne. Its owner was the husband of the infamous Madame Restell, New York's most notorious abortionist. In 1878, Anthony Comstock, the Jerry Falwell of his day, succeeded in driving the woman to suicide. Her grand mansion was then combined with the adjoining Osborne apartment house to become the Langham Hotel. Thomas Osborne evidently felt that he could safely ignore the previous use of the name, and he christened his new apartment venture after himself.

Osborne expected to turn a profit, and he thought his building's façade could help. As a stonemason, it was logical for Osborne to call for a stone front, and to help lure ex-brownstone-row-house residents, he decided upon the familiar look of brownstone for the outside of the building. Architect Ware fashioned the material into heavily rusticated blocks and manipulated the building's design so it would appear to be an Italian Renaissance palazzo. He put a large porchlike structure at the entrance and gave the entry portal a massive round arch with a fearsome carved head for a keystone. There were also three multiple-modillioned belt courses, each capped with a decorated stone balustrade, and a modest cornice at the roofline.

Reflecting the mezzanine arrangement at the rear of the apartments, the Seventh Avenue façade was subtly divided into two sections, with the northern one showing the 15 lower-ceilinged levels of subsidiary rooms. This dichotomy of façade treatment was also shown at the roof, with the cornice line originally stepping down at the north end of the structure. Later, however, this was raised to provide additional rooms at the top floor.

Reinforcing the feeling of massive solidity and impregnability, there was a balustraded moat around the building, bridged only at the entrance pavilion on West 57th Street. This moat served the same purpose as the front yard of the row house, separating the public domain from the private, with the entrance porch substituting for the stoop.

According to the pre-opening announcement article in the *Real Estate Record and Guide* of March 22, 1884, the building was to offer as additional inducements a private billiard room, the services in the basement of a resident doctor, a druggist and a florist, and, on the roof, a lawn for playing croquet. If the reporter is to be believed, the lawn would be shaded with blinds in the summer and would be enclosed and steam-heated in the winter, thus offering the important exercise opportunity of croquet-playing the year around. The article went on to claim that

> everything necessary to the comfort and health of such a large number of people who will reside in this large building will be provided for. It is claimed for this apartment house that it is designed with a view to the comfort and security of life rather than to ornamentation, and no one can pass by it without feeling that it is a very solid and substantially-built structure.

Not everyone looked upon the building's appearance with favor, however. On September 12, 1885, just two months before the first tenants moved in, the *Real Estate Record and Guide* criticized the façade, saying that the brownstone "is not well used," and that the design of the building's elements "is crude and unskillful." The magazine's writer summed up with the highly critical statement, "In fact, there is nothing architecturally interesting about the Osborne, except the grouping of the stories, and here and there some carving that is good in execution."

The criticism of the building's exterior may have been prompted by a perception that the nouveau-riche builder was overdoing things in what was "merely" a multiple-dwelling. The builder was certainly being lavish with the structure, but perhaps the greatest extravagance was reserved for the lobby, which was designed by the sculptor/painter Jacob Adolphus Holzer. The floor was laid with large slabs of vari-colored Italian marbles and set with paneled sections done in small mosaic tiles. The lower wall wainscots were complementary marble slabs with carved marble recesses and benches. Plaques, decorated with nude figures and floral garlands, were set into the wainscot at strategic intervals. Each was carved in plaster but finished to look like cast bronze. There was also a classically inspired cap frieze of more plaster carving and mosaic tiles. The upper walls were encrusted with still more carvings, tile work, and della Robbia–esque multicolored rondels. The massive interior arches were covered with similar decorations, and the ceiling was completely done in reds, blues and gold leaf in a shallow rendering of a deeply coffered Renaissance ceiling of the sort later used by J. P. Morgan in his private library on East 36th Street.

These expensive amenities were evidently more than Thomas Osborne could handle, and he was forced ultimately to declare bankruptcy and to give up his building. Osborne had purchased the land underlying his project in 1883 from one John Taylor for $210,000. The cost of the grand structure came to some $2 million, part of which had been loaned to Osborne by Taylor. Mortgages had been given by Osborne to

secure these loans, and when that debt could no longer be supported, the Taylor interests foreclosed, taking possession in 1888. The Taylor heirs were so successful in renting the Osborne's apartments that they found it expedient to expand the building in 1907 onto the 25-foot lot that separated the Osborne from the Art Students League.

Rather than create more individual units, the expansion merely added bedrooms to the extreme westerly apartments, with a few other alterations being done to those units as well. In finished form, each of those enlarged apartments had a reception room, 14 feet by 26 feet (*Figure 21*), a bigger dining room than before and seven bedrooms, in addition to the original parlor, library, kitchen and servants' rooms. The architects for the expansion were Julian Clarence Levi (who lived at the Osborne until his

Above: Figure 21. *The reception room in one of the westerly apartments of the expanded Osborne, as shown in a publicity photograph of 1910. (Collection of Andrew Alpern.)* Opposite: Figure 22. *The lobby of the Osborne, 1986, as restored by the Rambusch Studios and others for its cooperative tenant owners. (Bill Rothschild, courtesy of William Weber.)*

death in 1971 at 96) and Alfredo S. G. Taylor (an heir of John Taylor and a part owner of the building). The contractor for the work was the family firm of Taylor, Freeman, and Ely.

Although the building enjoyed prosperity for many years, it shared the fate of great numbers of grand old buildings whose surrounding neighborhoods changed. The increasing press of commercial needs in the area dictated the conversion in 1919 of the ground-floor space for shops, and the removal of the entrance porch and the protective moat. A shift uptown of the most fashionable residential areas made the Osborne's large apartments difficult to rent, and beginning in 1922 some of the apartments were subdivided to create smaller units. Changing living styles and further economic pressures led in 1941 to the conversion to individual apartments of the extra servants' rooms in the attic.

The Taylor family continued to hold the Osborne as an investment, but the depredations of neglected maintenance forced upon the building by the exigencies of rent regulations suggested that the building's useful life was coming to an end. Finally sold to a developer, in 1961 it faced demolition and replacement by a 17-story pile of boxy small apartments.

In a melodramatic rescue, it was saved just in the nick of time by the purchase of the building by its residents, and its conversion in 1962 to cooperative status. The Osborne's rebirth can be dated from that year, and although its exterior no longer looks like a restroom for pigeons or the inside of a fireplace flue, the disfigurements of the economically essential stores compromise the façade's attractiveness. Individual apartments have been rejuvenated by their owners, but the real glory is the restoration of the splendor of the original lobby. Although it had acquired over the years a uniformly dark brown patina of dirt and cigarette smoke, by what must have been a minor miracle the basic integrity of the 1885 decorations had not been compromised by the passing years. Craftsmen from the Rambusch Studios, along with other specialists, scrubbed off the dirt, polished the marble, repatinated the bronze and repainted and regilded, until the opulence again shone forth in all its magnificence *(Figure 22)*.

Today, the Osborne is once again home to those who are financially secure—those who choose to dwell in an atmosphere that is beyond replication, and in a neighborhood where creative activity and constant movement substitute for sylvan charms or reclusive repose.

Street. He may also have been responsible for design work on the limestone mansion of Louis Stern at 993 Fifth Avenue, now demolished.

For this new building, Stokes instructed Duboy to prepare sketches of an eclectic Beaux-Arts French *hôtel particulier,* but one blown up to Brobdingnagian proportions. (Exactly how much of the Ansonia's design was the product of Stokes, and how much was created by the academically trained and more architecturally experienced Duboy, is a matter for speculation. Stokes scholar Lori Zabar suggests that family records kept under wraps by W. E. D. Stokes, Jr. may some day shed light on that question.)

The façade was to be intricate and aggressively French. Everything was to be uninhibitedly lavish, sparing neither imagination nor expense. The result was massively spectacular: 17 stories of gleaming whiteness in limestone, brick and terra-cotta, manipulated into a giant wedding cake *(Figure 23).*

Especially French-looking were the three-story crested mansard roof and the rounded towers framing the Broadway façade. These corner sentinels were topped with high domes, capped by corbelled circular platforms and surmounted with turreted openwork-iron pavilions. The original design additionally called for a spectacular 11-story open stone tower at the center of the structure to serve as the visual *pièce de résistance,* but this was never built. As it would have been one of the last items to be constructed, and as the completion of the project was delayed almost three years by a series of labor disputes and by union jurisdictional unrest, mounting costs may have doomed it.

Stokes named his new project the Ansonia, after the community in Connecticut founded by his grandfather, Anson Greene Phelps. It was indeed grand and unusual. It was erected by Stokes's own construction firm, Onward Construction Company, named after a champion horse from the Stokes stable. The New York Architectural Terra-Cotta Company, also owned by the developer, provided masonry materials, and Stokes's Standard Plunger Elevator Company installed the six hydraulic passenger elevators and the separate service lifts.

The Ansonia was reported to have been the largest hotel in the world at its completion, comprising 122 housekeeping apartments and 218 nonhousekeeping units and transient quarters. Begun on November 15, 1899, construction was not officially finished until April 19, 1904. Nonetheless, by February 1903, there were 110 occupants living in the building. There were over 2500 rooms, along with an asserted 175 miles of

piping and conduit to carry electrical and telephone wires, pneumatically propelled messages, steam, and hot, cold and iced water to each of the suites.

Apartments ranged from modestly conventional bachelor flats to expansive suites that contained some of the most unusual rooms any multiple dwelling in the city had to offer. Parlors could be round, bay-windowed or even elliptical. Libraries had apsidal ends, hallways were oval or semicircular, and some of the bedrooms were shaped like heraldic shields. Servants' rooms were included within the apartments (a decided improvement over the unheated garrets in the Ansonia's antecedent apartment houses in France) and the layouts were flexible, allowing bedrooms to be added or subtracted with ease.

Entrance to the Ansonia was from a recessed carriage driveway on West 73rd Street, or through portals on West 74th Street and on Broadway. The ground floor contained reception rooms *(Figure 24),* a palm garden and an assembly room, as well as a large public dining room and a smaller grill room. An additional restaurant was located on the sixteenth floor, connected to a trellised roof garden. Tenants could avail themselves of any of these facilities, or could have meals sent up to their rooms. A theater, a grand ballroom and a large swimming pool were included, along with a garage, a barber shop, a florist, a druggist, a laundry, safe-deposit vaults and an electricity-generating plant. For a time, Stokes, who lived in the Ansonia's penthouse, provided the tenants with fresh eggs from chickens he housed on the roof. He also ran a small livestock farm at that high altitude, with pigs, goats, geese and ducks. This continued until 1907, when the city's health department claimed a Sanitary Code violation, and Stokes gave all the animals to the menagerie in Central Park.

Rents began at $600 a year and went up to ten times that amount for a 14-room suite with full hotel services. Over the years, many who paid those rates were in the music and entertainment industries: actresses Billie Burke and Mae Murray; singers Enrico Caruso, Fyodor Chaliapin, Geraldine Farrar, Bidú Sayão, Lily Pons, Lauritz Melchior, Ezio Pinza and Tito Schipa; impresarios Sol Hurok, Giulio Gatti-Casazza and Florenz Ziegfeld; and conductors Fausto Cleva and Arturo Toscanini.

The palmy days of the building lasted only a quarter of a century. As was the case with many of New York's grand old apartment houses, the Ansonia suffered the depredations of the Great Depression of the 1930s. The restaurants closed, the musicians left the roof

Opposite: Figure 23. *The Ansonia in 1904, when it was new and still had all of its glorious ornamentation. (Wurts Brothers, courtesy of the Museum of the City of New York.)*

garden and the live seals that once cavorted in the lobby fountain were sent to more congenial surroundings. The oriental rugs in the upstairs corridors disappeared, the elegant furniture in the public rooms was sold, and the large apartments were subdivided into more marketable units. According to Stokes historian Zabar, the grand ballroom was remodeled into the first indoor miniature golf course in the United States. The carriage driveway was blocked up, the lounges and lobbies converted to commercial use, and the Broadway street-level façade destroyed for stores.

The decline was exacerbated by the restrictions of the "temporary" (yet still extant) wartime rent-control laws. Maintenance chores were left undone and physical decay set in. The rooftop iron towers rusted and were removed, the copper crestings were sold for scrap, and deteriorating ornamentation was destroyed rather than being repaired *(Figure 25)*. The building changed hands several times and matters worsened. An invasion of predatory sneak thieves in the late 1960s prompted vigilante tenant groups to patrol the upstairs hallways armed with clubs and whistles.

Goaded into action in 1971 by rumors of impending demolition, the tenants finally began a vigorous campaign to have the Ansonia designated by the city as an official historic landmark. A long list of prominent New Yorkers endorsed their efforts, and a nostalgic reminiscence by an elderly man who had lived in the Ansonia from 1913 to 1954 appeared in the *New York Times*.

Landmark designation came in 1972, but did little to resolve the building's difficulties. Although exterior changes became subject to scrutiny by the Landmarks Preservation Commission, interior problems still remained unresolved. A new group of owners bought the structure and began an expensive program of repair and renovation. New howls of pain arose from the tenants, however, when the owners displayed aesthetic insensitivity with their alterations, and attempted to raise rents to pay for the long-deferred maintenance.

The tenants' association, and later a radical rival group, began a series of tactical lawsuits against the owners. These escalated into a bonanza for the lawyers, with a tenuous truce reached in 1989. The tenants agreed in principle to accept a condominium conversion of the building, although negotiations on the offering terms have yet to be completed. Until all the documents are signed and the conversion completed, the ultimate fate of the Ansonia remains in doubt. At the heart of the matter is more than half a century of neglect and repeated expedient alterations. Nonetheless, with some luck, the building may yet be "saved."

Opposite: Figure 24. *The lobby of the Ansonia in its heyday, ca. 1916. (Joseph Byron, courtesy of the Museum of the City of New York.)*
Below: Figure 25. *The south façade of the Ansonia about 1965, showing telltale scars where four decorative balconies were removed. (Charlotte LaRue.)*

Halfway Houses

Apartments aspiring to residential respectability

FOR YEARS AND YEARS, May 1 was the traditional "moving day" in New York. And the only abode suitable for a family with any social pretensions to move to was a one-family home: a brownstone, a limestone-fronted row house, a brick-terraced house, a freestanding mansion or even a simple timber-framed clapboard-fronted cottage on a narrow side street. But small or large, modest or grand, rented or owned, it had to be a structure under whose roof only a single family would dwell.

While living in a quality hotel was perfectly acceptable for anyone, and boardinghouse living was not *infra dig* for a single working man, a family dwelling in a tenement was socially beyond the pale (or, at the very least, well below the salt).

For the first 50 years of our existence as an independent nation, there were really very few available options for housing. Owning a home of whatever type was preferable, but single people or small families could share space in the house of another, with or without board included. There were old one-family houses (especially in crowded urban centers such as New York) that had been converted for use by several unrelated families. In such situations, plumbing was not a problem, since it simply did not exist; backyard privies were the only option (with chamber pots and low-level servants to tend them for the infirm). While there had always been taverns with sleeping rooms above, hotels as we know them did not exist until the 1830s. The Park Hotel, opened in 1836 at Broadway and Vesey Street, across from St. Paul's Chapel of the Trinity Parish, was among the first.

Designed by architect Isaiah Rogers for John Jacob Astor, common usage forced a name change almost immediately to the Astor House *(Figure 26).*

It was just about the same time that tenements built specifically for working families first appeared on the scene. Thus far, no one has determined conclusively which building was the very first, although an early contender was a four-story structure erected in 1833 on Water Street near Jackson Street. Built by Thomas Price and owned by James Allaire, it housed one family on each of its floors and qualified as a multiple dwelling. For more than a generation, however, a multiple dwelling carried strong connotations of low living and drunken brawls, or at least of social levels not to be associated with by those who considered themselves to be "proper."

Although apartment living had achieved social acceptance in Europe many years before, it was not until the fourth quarter of the nineteenth century that it began to be considered a "civilized" alternative to row-house living in New York. And even at that, its foundations were not really secure until World War I had changed almost every other aspect of proper society as well.

One particular element of an apartment that seemed to perpetuate its low status was the existence of all its rooms on a single level. Since all but the meanest hovels had at least two floors, a proper home required a vertical separation between entertaining spaces and the sleeping rooms, with the service spaces and servants even further removed. In an effort to ameliorate this disadvantage, developers of apartment house

Figure 26. *John Jacob Astor's new hotel of 1836 at Broadway and Vesey Street. (Collection of Andrew Alpern.)*

projects have sought—down to the present day—to design their offerings as "halfway" houses; as apartments that "feel" like one-family residences.

These fall into essentially four types of units: the "studio"; the multifloor duplex or triplex; the "duplexed" unit, or semiduplex; the "interlocked" unit.

The "studio" has nothing whatever to do with the tiny flat that housing hucksters in New York now call a studio (and those in England call a "bed-sitter"). The present-day studio is nothing more than a one-bedroom apartment without the bedroom—a dwelling of such minimal size that not even two livable and distinct rooms can be carved out of it.

The very first of the "real" studio apartments antedated apartments as we know them in New York, and were actually intended to be studios for real artists, with attached living quarters. The earliest such building known to have been erected for that purpose was the Studio Building at 51 West 10th Street, completed in 1858 to the designs of the French-trained American architect Richard Morris Hunt. It featured large double-height studios for painting, sculpture or design activities, each with attached apartment accommodations *(Figure 27).*

The project caught on immediately, with such luminaries as Frederick Church, Winslow Homer, John La Farge and William Merritt Chase maintaining residences there. Even Hunt used one of the units for many years as his home, his working architectural office and his classroom (he taught such aspiring younger architects as Frank Furness, George B. Post and William R. Ware). The building remained fully occupied until it was razed in 1956 to make way for a vastly more ordinary residential structure (which looks more like a huge filing cabinet than anything else). Although the Studio Building's units were grand, functional and irreplaceable, the structure was done in by still-extant rent regulations that made the enterprise economically viable only when destroyed.

The grandeur of a spectacularly high-ceilinged room has always been connected with a large free-standing house (and, generally, one located in England, Italy or France, to judge by the decorative details used in them). Thus, an apartment with such a space would be a "suitable" place to live even if the rest of its rooms were all on the same floor. It could be considered at least "halfway" a house.

The large "studio" living room, two stories high,

Figure 27. *The Studio Building of Richard Morris Hunt, continuing to function in 1936 as originally planned in 1858. (Berenice Abbott, courtesy of the Museum of the City of New York.)*

was quickly adopted by those whose connection to the arts related more to appreciation than to creation, and developers erected buildings containing such spaces. In some cases, the extra-height studio was attached to a single-floor apartment, as with 44 West 77th Street, designed by Harde & Short, and 51 Fifth Avenue, designed by Thomas W. Lamb.

In most cases, however, the studio room was part of a two-floor duplex suite. Architect Charles W. Buckham used that arrangement for the Gainsborough Studios (completed in 1908, and still standing in its restored glory at 222 Central Park South; *Figure 28*) and for the grand 471 Park Avenue *(Figure 29)*, whose steel framework is all that remains, hidden behind the

vacuous façade of the 1962 reconstruction of that splendid building. West 67th Street still houses a wondrously high concentration of these grand apartments, including the well-known Hotel des Artistes.

"Normal" duplex apartments (and even occasional triplexes) with conventional complements of rooms arranged on stacked levels have been the most widely used means of making an apartment feel more like a house. A staircase leading to upstairs bedrooms can make one almost expect to find a broad lawn directly outside the front door. Duplex units such as these were used first in the 1880s, and they have been used continually ever since, with even the most current offerings including duplexes.

Above, left: Figure 28. *The Gainsborough Studios of 1908 at 222 Central Park South: duplex apartments with two-story studios overlooking the park. (Wurts Brothers, courtesy of the Museum of the City of New York.)* Above, right: Figure 29. *471 Park Avenue in 1910, prior to its reconstruction. The windows of the double-height studio living rooms are accentuated on the façade; they combine with the majestic cornice and the pseudo entrance porch to create a grandeur now lost. (Wurts Brothers, courtesy of the Museum of the City of New York.)*

A logical (but only occasional) extension of the duplex-apartment-as-ersatz-house idea is the maisonette, in which the entrance to the apartment unit is directly from the street rather than through the apartment-house lobby or (worse yet) via an upstairs elevator hallway. William F. Buckley, Jr. lives in a maisonette at Park Avenue and East 73rd Street, but many similar apartments have been converted to more economically lucrative professional or commercial uses.

A true duplex, where the two portions of an apartment are stacked one directly on top of the other, is expensive to construct. The structural framework must be very carefully arranged, and the plumbing piping is far more complex, often requiring duplication of riser stacks and awkward offsets. A far less expensive alternative, which also offers the halfway feeling of a house, is the "duplexed," or semiduplex, unit.

A duplexed unit is essentially a conventional apartment in which the hallway leading to the bedrooms is replaced with a staircase. Thus, the apartment is on two floors, but the bulk of the additional architectural expense is avoided. Constructing the stairs is an extra cost, and the arrangements of the bottom floor and the top floor have to be different, but these extra bothers were considered to be minimal when the added marketing advantage of the more "homelike" atmo-

Figure 30. *The Brentmore, a 1910 apartment house at West 69th Street and Central Park West. Its duplexed units were a special selling point. (Courtesy of the Museum of the City of New York.)*

sphere needed 75 or 80 years ago was considered. The Brentmore, completed in 1910 at 88 Central Park West to the designs of Schwartz & Gross, used the duplexed principle for one-third of its apartments. Its advertising promoted this unusual feature by observing that it eliminated the objectionable aspect of ordinary duplex apartments, which necessitated a bedroom of one apartment being directly below the living room of another *(Figure 30)*.

A complex and architecturally expensive arrangement has been occasionally used over the years to lend distinction to apartment-house offerings by enabling the more "public" entertaining rooms of each unit to enjoy higher ceilings than the more private bedroom and service areas. This entails interlocking apartments on alternate floors. On one floor the living rooms would be at the front of the building with the bedrooms at the back. On the floor above, the higher-ceilinged living rooms would be at the back, with the bedrooms facing the front. Thus each pair of floors would encompass the same total vertical dimension, but that space would be divided between the apart-

ments in an interlocking manner that would benefit both units.

This was accomplished successfully in the 1920s by architects Pleasants Pennington and Albert W. Lewis at 66 East 79th Street, where the living and dining rooms of each 11-room full-floor apartment have 11-foot ceilings, with the bedrooms having more conventional 9-foot ones. The same scheme was employed 60 years later in a modern building at 525 East 80th Street by architect Bernard Rothzeid.

A century ago, apartment living was a new thing to New Yorkers, and financial imperatives required developers to design their apartment offerings in a way that would ease the transition from house-dwelling to flat-dwelling and that would make the aspiring apartments more residentially respectable. The architectural complexities of studios, duplexes, maisonettes and other special varieties helped their sales efforts. Today, developers still have to compete for buyers, and they have used similar techniques to create apartments that will turn a profit. *Plus ça change . . .*

Dramatic des Artistes

Sumptuous studios for aesthetic affluence
at One West 67th Street

FOR ALL ITS MUCH-VAUNTED and world-renowned sophistication and grandeur, New York City is (for New Yorkers, at least) a city of small neighborhoods and discrete (and often discreet) enclaves. The flower market branches off a short strip of Sixth Avenue in the 20s; diamond merchants and jewelers cluster on a single block of West 47th Street; East 70th Street has masses of splendidly preserved one-family houses; and West 67th Street is home to the world's greatest concentration of double-height studio apartments.

Between 1903 to 1919, six grand and distinctive studio buildings were erected on West 67th Street between Columbus Avenue and Central Park West. The entire concept was said to belong to artist Henry W. Ranger, called the "dean of American landscape painters" in his 1916 *New York Times* obituary. Ranger was said to have been irked at having to pay $700 a year for a suitable painting studio, as well as $2000 a year for an appropriate apartment to entertain friends and patrons. He envisioned a cooperative apartment building in which double-height studios enjoying northern light would be included within living quarters of suitable size and beauty. That was realized first in 27 West 67th Street, which opened in 1903. This cooperative featured large studios that were "pre-sold" to a group of "founders," as well as smaller apartments that the cooperative corporation could rent out in order to keep operating expenses down for the tenant-owners.

Joining Ranger as one of the building's original stockholders was Walter Russell, a self-taught painter, sculptor, musician and (in later years) educator and mystical scientist. Russell claimed, and has received, most of the credit for the cooperative studio/apartment house concept. Regardless of who started things off, however, it was Russell's zealous efforts that may be considered the driving force behind the West 67th Street studio enclave.

Several architects were used for the buildings, including B. Hustace Simonson, Rich & Mathesius, and Pollard & Steinam. George Mort Pollard dominated the group, though, and it was to him that Walter Russell turned for the design of the largest and most famous of the studios.

Dubbed the Hotel des Artistes, this building carries the address of One West 67th Street, and was to cover the six remaining vacant lots on the north side of West 67th Street *(Figure 31)*. Pollard's design drew heavily on Gothic antecedents *(Figure 32)* and included figural carvings representative of the arts *(Figure 33)*. The structure is 150 feet long, 150 feet high and extends practically the entire 100-foot depth of the property. Because of the existing building laws, the height—more than double the width of the street—meant that, as only hotels were permitted to be so tall, the amenities of a hotel would have to be provided: a communal kitchen, a large dining room, squash courts, a swimming pool *(Figure 34)*, a theater and a ballroom *(Figure 35)*. The last two elements now serve as supplementary studio space for the Capital Cities/ABC television center across the street, but the swimming pool is used regularly by the residents and the dining room is open to the public as a restaurant called the Café des Artistes.

Above: Figure 31. *Hotel des Artistes at One West 67th Street in 1989. The huge south-facing window enframements were designed to conceal the fact that some of them illuminated two-story living rooms while others served stacked rooms of ordinary height. (Andrew Alpern.)* Opposite, bottom: Figure 32. *Limestone decorative trim carved into an interpretation of Gothic forms, 1989. (Andrew Alpern.)* Opposite, top: Figure 33. *A frieze of jesterlike faces below the third-floor windows, and the chiseled face of an allegorical figure representing the art of architecture. (Andrew Alpern.)*

The Hotel des Artistes officially has only nine floors, but, with its mezzanine levels, it actually has twice that number. The majority of its apartments are duplexes with some distinctive double-height studios. One of the grandest was originally designed by architect William Tachau for philanthropist Aaron Naumburg. (Tachau later designed the Naumburg Band Shell in Central Park.)

Although the West 67th Street building was officially completed in February 1919, the work Tachau specified for the Naumburg suite was not finished and furnished until two years later. The double-height studios were ostensibly for working artists (albeit wealthy ones), but the brushes and paints were gone by the time Naumburg moved in *(Figure 36)*.

His "studio" was 54 feet long, with an 18-foot ceiling. Lavishly wood-paneled and hung with lush tapestries, it was surmounted by a wood-beamed roof

tracery and overlooked by a wood-balustraded balcony. Expensively done with antique Italian furniture, fine paintings and a profusion of exquisite oriental rugs, the studio was the centerpiece of an expansive terraced triplex apartment at whose pinnacle was a small Italian casino, or card room, lined with elaborately arcaded and extravagantly ornamented woodwork. With its carved figures, its Gothic trefoils, quatrefoils and traceries, and its leaded and stained-glass windows, the little room seemed more like a chapel than a garret for gambling at cards. (After Naumburg died, the paneling, furnishings and artwork of the entire ensemble of "public" rooms was recreated as an annex to the Fogg Museum in Cambridge.)

The apartment was subsequently owned by two other prominent and wealthy individuals. In 1932, author Fannie Hurst took it over, refurnished it and

Above, top: Figure 34. *The swimming pool of the Hotel des Artistes, ca. 1950. (Courtesy of Valerie Markwood.)* Above, bottom: Figure 35. *The ballroom of the Hotel des Artistes, ca. 1950. (Courtesy of Valerie Markwood.)* Opposite: Figure 36. *A small portion of the studio living room of Aaron Naumburg at One West 67th Street, 1919. (Avery Library, courtesy of Christopher Gray.)*

Figure 37. *The studio of one-time court painter Emil Fuchs, ca. 1920. (Courtesy of Christopher Gray.)*

lived in it until her death in 1968. It remained vacant—its windows dirty and its paint peeling—for six years, finally being sold for about $100,000 to its current occupant, Valerie Markwood, an artist who paints large and colorful canvases.

The apartment has finally fulfilled its original intent: the "studio" is now a Studio. Renovated under the guidance of architect Byron Bell, the original multipaned windows were replaced with huge expanses of glass whose light is tempered with adjustable vertical blinds. Lighting engineer Abe Feder installed four gargantuan ceiling light tracks and a theatrical rolling light tower for Markwood to direct onto her works-in-progress.

Over the years, the building's residents have represented substantial achievement in the visual and literary arts, in politics and in journalistic criticism. Many have left their mark. An upstairs tenant, the well-known artist Howard Chandler Christy, adorned the walls of the Café des Artistes with murals (which have been well maintained over the years) depicting three dozen shapely maidens cavorting *au naturel* among wooded glades and sylvan waters. It has been said that some of the models seen in the murals occasionally dined at the café (presumably more decorously draped) to the delight of the patrons who recognized them. Christy's depictions of sultry sirens and languorous lovelies in magazines and books earned for him such an impressive reputation as an authority of feminine pulchritude that he was named the sole judge for the first Miss America contest.

Matching Christy in popular appeal as a painter was resident Norman Rockwell. Portraitist Emil Fuchs, however, had a rather more elite clientele. He had been court painter to Queen Victoria and Edward VII, but by 1929 he was out of fashion and dying of cancer. Befitting his elegantly flamboyant and grand studio apartment *(Figure 37),* he chose to leave in an equally grand manner. He dressed carefully, donning a silk sash with his medals on it. Arranging portaits of his former royal patrons in a semicircle facing a fine old armchair, he sat down with a glass of the vintage port Queen Victoria had given to him. He took a little pearl-handled revolver inscribed to him by Edward, Prince of Wales, and then shot himself through the heart.

Although 1929 also saw a more sordid murder-suicide across the hall from Aaron Naumburg's suite, most of the residents of the des Artistes were not likely to find such dramatic notoriety. These included the explorers William Beebe and Roy Chapman Andrews, the dancer Isadora Duncan, film idol Rudolph Valentino, and writers Alexander Woollcott, Heywood Broun, Edna Ferber and Noël Coward. More recent occupants have been former Mayor John V. Lindsay, former Governor Hugh Carey, media manipulator David Garth and *New York Times* architecture critic Paul Goldberger *(Figure 38).*

Figure 38. *The apartment of David Garth as sublet temporarily by architecture critic Paul Goldberger, 1978. (Gil Amiaga.)*

Figure 39. *The original steel-and-glass marquee over the entrance as shown in an early publicity brochure, ca. 1950. (Courtesy of Valerie Markwood.)*

When the Hotel des Artistes was legally restructured as a modern cooperative in 1970, a number of residents purchased extra apartments. Some were combined, while others were retained as investments. Thus there is an unusually large number of long-term rental tenants—something not often found in an older co-op apartment building.

The original steel-and-glass marquee *(Figure 39)* has been replaced with a more conventional canvas awning *(Figure 40)*, and the stables and warehouses across the street have disappeared in favor of television studios and apartment houses, but the special ambience of the Hotel des Artistes remains. It is more than a quarter of a century since builder Walter Russell died, but if his ghost haunts the distinctive and dramatic building, he is probably satisfied to see that his masterpiece is still functioning as he had originally envisioned.

Figure 40. *The conventional awning that replaced the marquee, which someone thought looked old-fashioned. (Andrew Alpern.)*

Gotham Gothic

Theatricality and spaciousness at 44 West 77th Street

Above: Figure 41. *The Red House, at 350 West 85th Street, designed in 1903 by Harde & Short, in a view ca. 1906. (Wurts Brothers, courtesy of the Museum of the City of New York.)*
Opposite: Figure 42. *Original design rendering for 44 West 77th Street. (Courtesy of the Museum of the City of New York.)*

FOLLOWING UPON HIS INITIAL success with the studio/apartment concept on West 67th Street, but before he tackled the large and complex Hotel des Artistes, Walter Russell took the idea of extra-height studios to a 100-foot lot he had purchased on West 77th Street, opposite Manhattan Square and the expanding Museum of Natural History. He instructed the architectural firm of Harde & Short to develop an apartment design so distinctive and so unusual that it would be sure to attract buyers.

Formed in 1900, the partnership of Herbert Spencer Harde and R. Thomas Short was no stranger to the use of unusual historicism in apartment-house designs. In 1903 the firm designed The Red House at 350 West 85th Street *(Figure 41)* and, in 1906, the improbable 45 East 66th Street, both in the Elizabethan style. In 1908 the firm completed Alwyn Court, at 182 East 58th Street, which was garbed in a profusion of repetitive terra-cotta ornamentation *à la* Francis I.

For the West 77th Street project, Harde & Short mounted a two-pronged design campaign. The architects prepared a very unusual floor plan that included both "ordinary" large apartments and ones that included 1½-story, 600-square-foot studios. A special apartment with a double-height studio 44 feet long was created on the thirteenth floor for sculptor Karl Bitter.

The more visible aspect of the building's design, however, was the astounding façade *(Figure 42)*. Drawing freely from fifteenth-century Belgian civic

Above, left: Figure 43. *Gothic detailing abounded on the façade of 44 West 77th Street, 1909. (Wurts Brothers, courtesy of the Museum of the City of New York.)* Above, right: Figure 44. *The front of 44 West 77th Street as it originally appeared. (Wurts Brothers, courtesy of the Museum of the City of New York.)* Opposite: Figure 45. *The lobby of 44 West 77th Street, lacking only an altar to be a Gothic chapel, 1909. (Collection of Andrew Alpern.)*

architecture and from French church precedents, Harde & Short's building elevation was likened by one contemporary critic to a Gothic window in a Brobdingnagian cathedral. Encrusted with ornament that appeared to have been squeezed out of a pastry tube, there were Gothic and Tudor arches. There were crockets, finials, trefoils, quatrefoils and pinnacles. And there was enough tracery to satisfy even the Gothic historian-architect Viollet-le-Duc *(Figure 43)*.

While the architects and the developer may have been pleased with the results, architectural writers of the time were not very charitable. The critic of *The Architectural Record* called it "An Apartment House Aberration," and said that it made him stare and gasp in astonishment. Decrying the building's inappropriate scale, and pleading for a more generous expanse of

undecorated wall, the writer disdainfully asserted that the architect was merely rearing a monument to himself by erecting a "freakish front" *(Figure 44)*.

Although original Gothic ornamentation of the Middle Ages was carved in stone, all of the decoration on 44 West 77th Street above the second floor was executed in terra-cotta, colored to look like stone. Completed in 1909, the work was evidently imperfectly done. Less than two years later, a scaffold had to be erected the full height of the building to enable the loose fired-clay units to be reanchored to the supporting structure, and to permit all the joints to be repointed with new mortar. The stone-masonry industry, weakened by the increasing use of substitute materials, was quick to pounce on the problem and to publicize it widely.

The poor installation job, exacerbated by the acidity of the atmosphere and the damage caused by thousands of pigeons, ultimately proved irreparable, and in 1945 the "restoration" contracting firm of Nicholson & Galloway hacked off all the decorative terra-cotta features.

Forty-four West 77th Street offered amenities that are unknown today but were not especially unusual then. One of the much-touted advantages of apartment living was the availability of food services within the building and a communal dining room for parties or for regular meals. The Dakota had been built with extensive cooking and eating facilities; those at West 77th Street were more modest, comprising a single dining room operated in connection with the restaurant of the hotel next door. This feature was said to be especially attractive since it obviated a kitchen on the premises and the attendant fumes and odors. When the novelty of this arrangement wore off, however, the concept was abandoned and the food-service space on the ground floor was converted to a professional suite.

Above the second story, there were only two apartments per floor. Because of the extra-height studios, two of each vertical stack of three apartments included these extra rooms, the remaining unit having only the 18-by-27-foot living room, but not the high-ceilinged studio. All apartments, however, had four bedrooms, a library and three baths. The decorative features were (and generally still are) exceptionally lavish. The lobby is especially Gothic in feeling, with a groin-vaulted ceiling and a decorative balconied mezzanine *(Figure 45)*. The units themselves are elaborately wood-paneled and have suspended gessoed Venetian lanterns in the studios. There are carved-wood pilasters with Corinthian capitals, bronze-framed and leaded-glass doors, and decorated Caen stone fireplace mantels. Harde & Short's effort to create an ambience more lavish than a conventional row house appears to have been a resounding success, notwithstanding the early criticism in the architectural press.

In its original conception as a cooperative venture, more than half of the apartments were occupied by stockholders of the building's ownership corporation, with income gained from the rental of the remaining units. In the absence of the current restrictions of the Internal Revenue Service, this was a common arrangement in the early days of cooperative apartment houses.

During the Great Depression of the 1930s, large, expensive apartments were a drug on the market, with few people able to afford them. Sharing the fate of many other grand old buildings, 44 West 77th Street had its mortgage foreclosed, and the financial structure was converted to a conventional rental arrangement.

Reflecting a much-changed economic environment, the units were resold as cooperatives in 1970. In today's market it seems incredible, yet at that time the largest apartment in the building, the 11-room suite on the thirteenth floor, with the extra-size studio, sold for $57,000, with a monthly maintenance of $617. Occupied since the 1930s by portrait artist Paul Trebilcock, the apartment was sold by his widow's estate in 1988 for over $3 million. The maintenance had then reached $2,200 a month. *Sic transit gloria pacti pretio!*

Commodious Courtyards

An escape from the Manhattan street grid

URBAN LIVING HAS ALWAYS engendered conflicting feelings. On the one hand, New Yorkers revel in being at the epicenter of activity, in cavorting within the world's culture capital, in being surrounded by sumptuous shopping and admirable architecture. On the other hand, they seek quiet amid the bustle, a bit of respite from the frantic activities of the day, a sense of individuality in their homes.

Those who enjoy the mixed pleasures of brown-stone-row-house living in the city can obtain that feeling of *rus in urbe* by having a modest front yard or front stoop, and some sort of rear garden. In its most rarified form, a brownstone backyard can be designed to transport its occupants to a world spiritually light years away from the frantic city.

But what of those who elect to live in an apartment house? Isn't there a compromise? This question was addressed as early as a century ago, and repeatedly

Above: Figure 46. *The Dakota, at West 72nd Street and Central Park West, ca. 1895. (Courtesy of the Museum of the City of New York.)* Opposite: Figure 47. *The inner courtyard of the Graham Court apartments as it originally appeared ca. 1901. (Wurts Brothers, courtesy of the Museum of the City of New York.)*

since then, with the answer coming in the form of courtyard apartments.

The courtyard version of the multifamily dwelling does two things: It seeks to provide a buffer zone between the "public" sidewalk and the "private" entrance, and it attempts to approximate the brownstoner's backyard as a place of escape.

A problem inherent in this concept is that it can be accomplished only when there is an unusually large plot available on which to erect the building. The nature of apartment-house planning makes it almost an impossibility on anything less than a full-block site, or at least on land that fronts on three streets at once. Since assembling land in New York is difficult, opportunities for courtyard buildings have arisen rarely. The problem has been exacerbated by the need to obtain maximum return on the land investment by offering as many apartment units in the structure as possible.

Because of these factors, there are very few courtyard apartment houses in New York. Many structures on sites as small as 75 feet by 100 feet have pathetic open spaces in their centers that are *called* courtyards but are really nothing more than enlarged air shafts. A

true courtyard building, in its purest form, provides an open landscaped space in the center, and arranges the entrances and elevator lobbies so they are reached by traversing the courtyard.

The first of these courtyards was the one surrounded by the stacked apartments of the venerable Dakota, at One West 72nd Street. Designed by Henry Janeway Hardenbergh (1847–1918), the building was originally erected in 1884 as a rental investment property by Singer Sewing Machine magnate Edward Clark *(Figure 46)*. While not particularly spacious, the Dakota's interior courtyard does provide access for carriages (cars had been invented only a few years earlier and were not used for normal transportation). It was designed as a decorative and landscaped space, and through it one can gain entrance to the four separate elevator lobbies serving the building. And it still serves the social needs of Dakota residents for parties and caroling at Christmas time.

Similar in concept, although larger in size and different in appearance, is the courtyard constructed as an integral part of the Graham Court Apartments *(Figure 47)*. This large and once-elegant building was built in 1901 at Seventh Avenue and West 116th

Above, top: Figure 48. *The Van den Heuval mansion of 1759 on the site of the Apthorp Apartments in 1903. (Courtesy of The New-York Historical Society.)* Above, bottom: Figure 49. *The architects' original design rendering for the Apthorp. (Courtesy of The New-York Historical Society.)* Opposite: Figure 50. *The inner courtyard of the Apthorp, ca. 1965. (Charlotte LaRue.)*

Street as an investment by William Waldorf Astor, even though he was living permanently in England.

Harlem at the turn of the century was a very upper-middle-class area, filled with professionals and businessmen living primarily in brownstone row houses. Astor hoped to lure them away from their private houses into apartments by providing a grand Italian Renaissance palazzo. He sweetened the offering by including a spacious landscaped entrance courtyard. Astor's concept worked, and despite the harsh realities of Harlem today, the building remains occupied and maintains an ongoing battle to keep the forces of decay and destruction at bay.

Seven years after completing Graham Court, Astor repeated this success by expanding its concept, and reproducing it in a far more grand and elegant form at the corner of West 79th Street and Broadway. He was able to purchase the block-square property in a single

transaction, acquiring with it the 1759 mansion of John C. Van den Heuval, which had become Burnham's Tavern in 1839 and had since fallen into a state of considerable disrepair *(Figure 48)*.

Using the services of architects Clinton and Russell, the team that had worked on the 116th Street project, Astor supervised an architectural masterpiece. He named it the Apthorp, after a road, mansion and family prominent in the history of the West Side *(Figure 49)*. The entire façade of the building is faced in limestone and is classically carved and rusticated, this treatment extending even to the courtyard façades. That inner space is elegantly detailed, with elaborate wrought ironwork, a pair of fountains, marble benches, statuary and greenery *(Figure 50)*. Entrance to the four elevator lobbies is gained via the pathways of this gracious courtyard.

Emulating the successes of Astor at 116th Street

Opposite, top: Figure 51. *The Belnord, West 86th Street and Broadway, 1908. (Irving Underhill, courtesy of the Museum of the City of New York.)* Above: Figure 52. *The huge courtyard of the Belnord, 1908. (Wurts Brothers, courtesy of the Museum of the City of New York.)* Opposite, bottom: Figure 53. *The courtyard of 1185 Park Avenue, designed by Schwartz & Gross, 1937. (Wurts Brothers, courtesy of the Museum of the City of New York.)*

and at 79th Street, the Belnord Realty Company erected a similar but far larger structure on the plot of vacant land at Broadway and West 86th Street *(Figure 51)*. Designed by architect H. Hobart Weekes and completed in 1908, the Belnord boasted the largest interior court in the world—94 feet wide by 231 feet long—and an underground delivery tunnel for trucks and wagons reachable via a ramped driveway from West 87th Street *(Figure 52)*. Architecturally nowhere near as successful as the Astor buildings, the Belnord, with its vast number of very large apartments, did not reach full occupancy until World War II. Since then, however, it has never had a vacancy for long, but has been embroiled for years in an acrimonious battle between its tenants and the building's elderly and eccentric owner.

Nearly as large is the grand courtyard building of 1929 at 1185 Park Avenue *(Figure 53)*. Erected by the prolific Bricken Construction Company to a design by

the even more prolific architectural firm of Schwartz & Gross, this hollow-square structure surrounds a large landscaped court that leads to six separate elevator lobbies, each serving no more than two apartments per floor, some of which are exceptionally large duplex penthouses. The building's architectural design treatment is superficially Gothic, centering visually on the triple-arched entrance to the courtyard from Park Avenue *(Figure 54)*. Even its smallest apartments are graciously spacious, but its unusual courtyard gives the building an aura of grandeur lacking in most of its neighbors.

Courtyard apartment houses are not unique to New York, but they have a special feeling that makes the few that have been built here unusually desirable, and they add an amenity to apartment-house living that enhances the pleasure of dwelling in what many consider to be the center of the civilized world.

Figure 54. *The block-long, vaguely Gothic apartment house at 1185 Park Avenue, 1937. (Berenice Abbott.)*

Lexington Luxury

Affluent living adjoining Gramercy Park
at One Lexington Avenue

HISTORICALLY, MANHATTAN BEGAN AS a Dutch town, but more than 300 years ago it was taken in the name of the English Crown. During the period of those 300 years, that conquest has shaped our laws, our thinking, our social customs, our decorative and architectural styles and our city planning.

We lack the street configurations of those European cities that were once walled-in and fortified. Other than a couple of pathetic attempts in Brooklyn and the Bronx, we do not have the grand boulevards that are the pride of cities such as Paris and Vienna. Despite our early origins, we do not possess the canals found in Amsterdam or in Venice. And while Manhattan's linear form has had a strong impact on its development, the ideal toward which New Yorkers have always aspired has been English, and especially what is to be found in London.

What is more evocative of the London of Wellington Square, Cadogan Gardens, Eton Place or Belgrave Square than this: a modestly sized, fenced-in residential minipark surrounded by discreet homes with lavishly comfortable interiors?

It was our century under English rule that established our mental mind set, but it was the civilized practicality and elegance of the English approach to urban living that maintained our predilection for British building habits long after George Washington had replaced George III as our head of state.

Samuel Bulkley Ruggles was born many years after America had declared its independence from the Crown, yet his cultural heritage was clearly English. He graduated from Yale at 14, and about seven or eight years later moved to New York. He married and began to practice law with considerable success. He was even more successful, however, in his real-estate investments.

By 1830, he found it more profitable to devote himself full time to the purchase and development of land, utilizing to the fullest his enlightened sense of how the city would probably grow, along with his obvious respect for English planning principles.

In 1831, he bought 23 pieces of property and prepared a plan for their development. Using the London residential square as a model, he designed a private park surrounded by lots ample enough for substantial row houses. He stipulated that the buildings were to be brick or stone and at least three stories high. Late that year, Ruggles deeded the land for the park in perpetuity to a group of trustees who were bound forever to maintain it for the benefit of the owners of the houses surrounding the park. Thus was Gramercy Park born.

Over the next few years, this private enclave and its surrounding streets were constructed, and the lots fronting the park were prepared for sale to "suitable" people.

At the same time, Samuel Ruggles recognized that Third and Fourth Avenues, intended as north–south arteries on the Commissioners' Street Map of 1811 (which established the grid plan by which Manhattan was developed), were insufficient to meet the needs of his new residential development (or of the rapidly expanding city, for that matter). Accordingly, he petitioned the local government to open an additional

Figure 55. *The adjoining houses of the Field brothers combined by Stanford White into a grand mansion for Henry Poor at the head of Lexington Avenue, ca. 1900. (Courtesy of the Museum of the City of New York.)*

avenue, offering a deed for that portion of the needed land that passed through his own propery. The civic bureaucracy recognized Ruggles' vision, accepted his proposal and laid out the new avenue. It was named for the Battle of Lexington, the first encounter between royal and rebel troops and the beginning of the American Revolution.

Lexington Avenue began at the north side of Gramercy Park, but it was not the first portion of the Ruggles land to be developed. In the 1840s, several very fine houses had been built along the western side. At one corner was a chaste residence designed by Alexander Jackson Davis, while adjoining were four charming houses, luxuriantly ornamented with foliated cast-iron entrances and verandas, two of which survive.

In 1847, the western corner of Lexington Avenue and East 21st Street was developed for Alexander M. Lawrence, a merchant and shipowner. Following the death of Lawrence, his brownstone-fronted house was extensively remodeled by architect Stanford White,

who lived in it from 1900 until his death in 1906 at the hands of the crazed playboy Harry K. Thaw.

The opposite corner, then known as 123 East 21st Street, remained vacant until 1852, when a house was completed on the site for inventor-businessman Cyrus West Field, who successfully supervised the laying of the first communications cable across the Atlantic Ocean in 1858. The house, an Italianate brownstone of the most up-to-date style, was erected with an adjoining twin at 125 East 21st Street for Field's brother.

Directly to the north, at 9 Lexington Avenue, the eminent philanthropist-industrialist Peter Cooper had erected his huge mansion, also in the popular Italianate mode. That house was remodeled in 1885 by Stanford White for Cooper's son-in-law, Abram Hewitt, one-time mayor of New York City.

The two Field families, meanwhile, were running back and forth between their respective homes quite regularly. In fact, it soon became expedient to connect their buildings by piercing the common party wall for a doorway. This connection was expanded by Stanford White when Henry W. Poor purchased the two houses.

The reconstruction for Poor turned the connected row houses into a single grand residence *(Figure 55)*. The entrance was moved to the ground floor and around the corner to Lexington Avenue, and, while the building remained relatively restrained on the outside, its interiors were reconstructed and redecorated with a lavishness of the Medici-like standard then *de rigueur* for successful princes of commerce. A new drawing room was created across the entire park frontage of the double house, a grand stairhall built and the interior ornamented with luxurious materials and lavish furnishings. Protecting the Poor mansion was a dry moat and an elegantly simple high iron fence of closely spaced and sharply pointed pickets. When the house was demolished in 1909, a bare eight years after it had been completed, it was only the moat and the fence that were saved, along with the address, One Lexington Avenue.

A year following, in 1910, a majestic 12-story apartment house was completed on the site Field had purchased 60 years before. The new structure retained the dry moat, the elegant iron fence and the aristocratic address, but it replaced the nineteenth-century concept of the one-family house with that of the twentieth-century multiple dwelling *(Figure 56)*.

Figure 56. *The replacement for the Poor house, the present One Lexington Avenue, 1910. (Irving Underhill, courtesy of the Museum of the City of New York.)*

Figure 57. *A preliminary design sketch of 1912 for a tunnel under Gramercy Park that never was built. (Courtesy of Mark Tomasko.)*

One Lexington Avenue was cooperatively owned from the start. It was erected by a company headed by Edward Corning with the object of providing homes in the building for each of the company's 12 owner-directors. The remaining apartments were to be leased out, and that income would help keep the maintenance costs of the owners' apartments as low as possible.

Architect Herbert Lucas' design is refined and restrained, with a two-story stone base and upper floors of a deep red brick laid in Flemish bond—an expensive subtlety. He provided voluted stone keystones over each window, as well as cast-iron balconies on stone console brackets, and a colonnaded and balustraded stone porch.

Lucas was a skillful designer. His building appears to be completely symmetrical and consistent at all levels. Concealed within the rhythmic façade, however, is a great deal of variety, reflecting the many variations in the apartments within.

The architect had to contend with the individual requirements of each of the 12 building owners, and also had to accommodate the wishes of those rental tenants who were willing to sign leases while the building was in the planning and early construction stages. To his credit, Lucas was able to create internal individuality without doing aesthetic damage to the exterior of the building, hiding those distinctions from all but the most critically observant passersby.

Most of the apartments were duplexes, with a few exceptions. Since the corner of Lexington Avenue fronting on Gramercy Park provided the most desirable units, these were reserved for the original cooperative owners. The most elaborate one, at the top of the building, had a two-storied salon.

While the building was still under design study, Lucas proposed that its accessibility be improved with the provision of a vehicular tunnel under Gramercy

Park to connect Lexington Avenue with Irving Place to the south. He produced a rough sketch of what he had in mind, in which he showed an approximation of his new apartment house *(Figure 57)*. However, his drawing also took some curious liberties with the realities of the surrounding neighborhood. The drawing showed the old City College building as being on East 22nd Street, when it was actually a block further north, and it omitted the Cooper-Hewitt house that should have been shown there. It showed a nonexistent suspension bridge in the background, and in the center of Gramercy Park it indicated a statue within a temple-like structure. The present statue of Edwin Booth was not erected until 1918, and at that point in the park there was a fountain instead. What Lucas drew there in place of the fountain looks curiously like the protective enclosure and statue of Peter Cooper which stands just to the south of Cooper Union. Was this merely a coincidence? Adding to the fantasy appearance of the drawing was the proposed tunnel itself. For it to work, Lexington Avenue and Irving Place, including their sidewalks, would have had to be at least 15 feet wider than they were. That may be why the plan evidently never went further than Lucas' original sketch.

Today, One Lexington Avenue is completely cooperative, with apartments changing hands only rarely. Each of its residents has access to the private and restricted Gramercy Park, and their guests have the privilege of special rates at the Gramercy Hotel directly across the avenue on the site of Stanford White's old home. One Lexington Avenue is well maintained, and has most of its mechanical systems and original fabric still intact and functioning. With its quietly elegant atmosphere and attentive staff, it is no wonder it is considered to be "Luxury on Lexington."

Faux French

The ersatz Beaux-Arts St. Urban at 285 Central Park West

THE DEVELOPMENT OF MANHATTAN started at the southern end of the island and gradually moved northward, with commercial occupancy generally pushing residential construction ahead of it. The front line extended more or less evenly across from the Hudson to the East River. But when the huge obstacle of Central Park was reached, real-estate speculation veered sharply to the right and continued relentlessly up the East Side. The West Side remained a virtual wasteland of squatters, shanties, old frame dwellings, open fields and rock outcroppings.

It was not until the elevated railway brought rapid transit to the West Side in 1879 that real-estate developers recognized the potential of this immense area. With ready accessibility to Riverside and Central Parks, the West Side offered sufficient space for accommodating the families of the expanding merchant and professional middle class.

The arrival of the el coincided with the restoration of confidence following the financial panic of 1873, and set the stage for the first tentative investments of speculative builders. By 1885, there were a few terraces of brick or brownstone row houses scattered about the area, mainly around the elevated railway stations along Ninth Avenue. As these houses were sold, more were built, and the area began to be considered a neighborhood. The new neighbors soon started pressing politicians for improvements, such as the renaming of Eighth Avenue in 1889 as Central Park West.

But what sort of Central Park West was it? There were the grand Dakota apartment house at West 72nd

Street, the original San Remo and Beresford apartment hotels, a few modest five-story blocks of flats and some row houses. Of the last-named, the most impressive was the block-long group of nine erected between West 84th and West 85th Streets to the designs of Edward Angell (*Figure 58*). The Dakota and the northern three houses of Angell's group are still standing; almost everything else is gone.

By 1891, the neighborhood was almost complete. There were only three vacant blocks on Central Park West north of West 66th Street. The rest were built solid with five-to-eight-story apartment houses, apartment hotels and well-constructed brownstones. But there were institutional structures, as well, including the innovative (and still extant) New York Cancer Hospital at the West 106th Street end and the vast American Museum of Natural History within the four-block Manhattan Square.

The streetscape was also enhanced by three churches and a synagogue. The latter, completed in 1897, served a group of Sephardic Jews whose ancestors came from Spain and Portugal. Since their congregation had been founded in 1654, they considered themselves to be the Jewish elite, and they looked down upon other Jews who had come to America during the nineteenth century, notably those from Germany. But those later German Jews prospered and made up a significant portion of the market for the spacious brownstones going up all over the West Side. Their families tended to be large, and required the expansive accommodations of the new row houses. They appreciated the solid bourgeois comforts these homes provided, as

Figure 58. *A view ca. 1890 showing the block-long row of one-family houses on Central Park West designed by Edward Angell. The three at the right are still standing. (Collection of Andrew Alpern.)*

indicated by the *Real Estate Record and Guide* of that period:

> These latter are built of limestone and brick. The vestibules occupy the full width and are of marble. Each house has an electric elevator. Billiard rooms, parquet floors, parlors and music rooms in white enamel and gold, are attractive features. A separate servants' staircase runs from cellar to roof. Kitchens have parquetry floors, French ranges and gas ranges, ovens and broilers. Cook pantries have glass-lined storage refrigerators, butlers' pantries have wine refrigerators, silver safes, and steam heated plate warmers.

The amenities were all that "modern technology" and artistic craftsmanship could produce. They contributed to the warm, friendly, and *gemütlich* home atmosphere the Germans liked so much. But *Gemütlichkeit* was needed elsewhere as well.

The Progress Club had provided warmth to German Jews since its establishment in 1864. Recognizing the West Side's emergence as the residential neighborhood of choice of many potential members, the club purchased the northern corner of West 88th Street and Central Park West in 1901, selected architect Louis Korn through a competition, and built a clubhouse to his Italian Renaissance palazzo design. This foursquare limestone structure emulated the much grander and more refined designs of the establishment architectural firm of McKim, Mead & White, but lacked the elegance and grace that the more skillful firm was able to bring to its commissions. Eclipsed by the more socially secure Harmonie Club (which had retained Stanford White's firm for its own East 60th Street clubhouse), the Progress Club passed out of existence in 1932, and its building was sold to the progressive Walden School. The school altered and expanded its building over the years, finally selling the

Figure 59. *The French-styled St. Urban at 285 Central Park West, ca. 1909. (Courtesy of Christopher Gray.)*

site to a developer for a tall apartment tower that was completed in 1989 and houses the school on its lower floors.

Shortly after the new Progress Club building was completed in 1904, construction began on the remaining open site immediately to the north. Merchant Peter Banner purchased the property and hired architect Robert T. Lyons to design an apartment house. Other than the 1884 Dakota and the Langham (which was then under construction on the blockfront from West 73rd to West 74th Streets), the only apartment houses on Central Park West were modest affairs. They contained units whose planning and decoration were far from ideal.

Since apartment living was still associated in the public's mind with France (where it was far more acceptable than it was in provincial New York), and since things French were considered generally to be au courant and chic, Banner elected to have his new venture designed in the French mode. He evidently felt that there was an affluent local market for grandiose French flats—the same market that was renting or buying the row houses that were ubiquitous on the West Side.

The traditional architectural elements of the French Second Empire were fair game at a time when high-rise apartment-house design was in its infancy and architects were willing to experiment in almost any style. Assembled and manipulated in a way advocated by the École des Beaux-Arts of Paris, these features were used by architect Lyons to create an overblown private mansion or *hôtel particulier (Figure 59).*

Sitting on a three-story rusticated limestone base, the building has a balustraded belt course separating the base from the body, and another marking the beginning of the upper portion. The massive mansard roof is pierced by elaborately pedimented dormer windows, and a circular tower surmounted by a dome

Figure 60. *The grand and unusual open carriage driveway of the St. Urban, ca. 1909. (Courtesy of Christopher Gray.)*

with round *œil-de-bœuf* windows marks the 89th Street corner. The building is crowned by a turreted cupola.

The building's entrance at 285 Central Park West is via a recessed carriage driveway that is no longer used for vehicles *(Figure 60)*. This entry leads to an elegantly furnished and decorated lobby, which in turn opens onto two elevator–stair halls, each serving two banks of apartments.

The building was dubbed the St. Urban, and its design so pleased the architect that he replicated its façade—complete with mansard, corner tower and turreted dome, but on a much larger scale—for a proposed hotel that was planned in 1908 for Grand Army Plaza in Brooklyn, but was never built.

Conventional marketing strategies then, as now, called for a mix of apartment sizes in a building to appeal to a broad range of potential residents. Peter Banner, through his architect, was singularly narrow-minded in identifying his market, however. Instead of a variety of apartment sizes, he offered but one.

Each unit had a "public" section with a living room, a library, a dining room and a foyer, all connected *en suite.* In three of the four units on each floor, the living and dining rooms were identical in size, and were separated from each other by a library. The dining and living rooms sported bay windows, nonworking fireplaces and spacious areas for entertaining. These suites were set at the front of each apartment, contrary to the more customary planning of the time, and they enjoyed sunlight and park views. In each unit there were also four good-sized master bedrooms, two baths, a kitchen, a pantry, two maids' rooms and a maids' bathroom.

The basement had private storage rooms for the tenants, quarters for the superintendent and room for the heating, lighting, refrigeration and power-supply apparatus. Additional machinery was provided to filter all incoming water.

The primary rooms and hallways of each unit were finished with parquet flooring, hardwood trim and specially designed hardware. The dining rooms featured quartered oak with paneled walls and beamed ceilings. The living rooms and libraries had mahogany details and the bedrooms were skirted with white enamel. The main bedroom in each apartment was fitted with a built-in wall safe, and the bathrooms and kitchens were furnished with the latest in fixtures and equipment. A tile-lined refrigerator in each kitchen was connected to a refrigeration plant in the basement. This permitted each apartment to make its own ice, which was quite a novelty at that time.

The St. Urban was said to have cost Banner $800,000, not including equipment or the land. He completed the building early in 1906 and hoped to rent at annual prices ranging from $3000 to $4500. He evidently overextended himself, however, and defaulted on the mortgage. The building was bought at a foreclosure sale by a lawyer, Albert Forsch, for $1,130,000. Forsch in turn sold it in August 1906 to the Barstun Realty Company, which rented out the units.

The officers of the Progress Club were apparently correct in their assessment of the ethnic make-up of the neighborhood. Lists of residents of the building for 1915 include many German-Jewish names, mostly merchants, manufacturers or professionals.

The St. Urban has not been a stranger to notoriety and controversy. It has long operated as a cooperative, and its stockholder-residents banded together in 1987 in an unsuccessful attempt to obtain official landmark status for the adjoining former Progress Club. Trying futilely to block the building's high-rise replacement tower, the residents were motivated at least in part by the potential loss of park views from their southern windows. They were ultimately rebuffed by New York's Landmarks Preservation Commission, which pointed to the 1958 removal of the club building's massive cornice and the addition of a fifth floor by the school.

A cornice had figured in an earlier controversy. In 1905, even before the St. Urban was completed, attorneys for the Progress Club filed a lawsuit against Peter Banner arguing that the cornice at the top of the southern wall encroached upon their air space and caused rainwater to drip onto the northern portion of their roof garden, reducing its usefulness.

During the construction of Banner's building there was a partial collapse of the structure. Although no one was killed, the incident caused the builder much grief and may have contributed to his ultimate loss of the building.

The St. Urban is a splendid anachronism, an irreplaceable and elegant receptacle of large and gracious apartments. Its Beaux-Arts design is representative of many of the important structures of its time, and it serves to mark much of what was best about the days before World War I.

The much-published architecture critic Ada Louise Huxtable grew up in the St. Urban, and has said of it, "Its style and substance were light years away from today's architectural con-game known as the 'luxury' apartment house." While its design and construction are from a past era, its reality remains. Even those who are not privileged to live in it nonetheless benefit from the graceful contribution of the St. Urban to the streetscape of the city.

Parisian Prasada

Spacious solidity at 50 Central Park West

MANHATTAN'S UPPER-MIDDLE-CLASS families of the 1850s, 1860s and 1870s lived in brownstone row houses that were solid, substantial and spacious. But they were also exhaustingly tedious to maintain. With rooms stacked vertically on narrow lots, the nineteenth-century brownstone entailed a significant amount of stair-climbing. Climbing two or three flights laden with the accoutrements of nonelectric cleaning cannot have been pleasant. And with the kitchen in the basement and the dining room on the first floor, even mealtimes involved a lot of walking.

The day-to-day running of the household was, of course, up to the wife, who might have been called the *châtelaine* if she had enough servants to help her. And servants were certainly needed. If heat or hot water was wanted, a boiler in the cellar would have to be stoked regularly with coal, and vast quantities of ashes just as regularly removed. The chilling of food called for periodic deliveries of large blocks of ice for the zinc-lined iceboxes, and wood was needed for the fireplaces and the kitchen stoves. Fresh food was delivered each day from a string of specialized merchants, and messenger boys abounded, since a telephone or telegraph connection in a home was a rarity. Even the most ordinary of middle-class living was no easy matter.

But change was gradually making itself felt. Paris, famous for its lavish and elegant apartment houses, served as the city to which architects of early New York apartment houses looked for inspiration. The size of those projects grew, as did the scope of their amenities. Building by building, developers were convincing New Yorkers of substance that a private

row house was not the only possible place in which a family could be properly raised.

During the 1870s, the still-new Central Park was being ornamented with such grand additions as the Bethesda Terrace and Fountain, the Dairy, the Belvedere and most of its picturesque pedestrian bridges. These elements enhanced a visit to the park and encouraged the development of the streets and neighborhoods bordering on it.

The vagaries of social imperatives tended to put the grander private dwellings to the east of the park, with the smaller row houses and the nascent apartment houses on the West Side. The opening of the Ninth Avenue Elevated Railway in 1879 further encouraged this trend, making the West Side immediately convenient to those whose social standing neither called for nor financially permitted the keeping of a carriage and horses.

Real-estate speculators and developers were quick to recognize this, one of the first major projects being Edward Clark's huge and lavish Dakota. Clark died before his project was finished, but when the Dakota opened in the autumn of 1884, it was obvious that Eighth Avenue would become one of the city's preeminent boulevards. Land speculators gobbled up every site along the avenue that could be had and then let them sit fallow, waiting for values to rise. Asking prices were generally too high for private houses, so cheaper land on the side streets was used for massive amounts of brownstone construction. Block after block of empty lots facing directly on the park remained dotted with old frame dwellings and the shacks and shanties of squatters, but around the

Figure 61. *The Prasada, 50 Central Park West, in its original mansard-roofed form, ca. 1909. (Irving Underhill, courtesy of the Museum of the City of New York.)*

corners the brownstones and their prosperous residents were creating a neighborhood presence conducive to rising land prices.

As values rose, the first growth of apartment houses and family-type hotels appeared, most to the north of Manhattan Square. The major blocks south of the American Museum of Natural History, however, remained open and undeveloped. It was probably the Hotel Majestic, which opened in 1892 just south of the Dakota, that really put the newly renamed Central Park West on the map.

The Majestic was not just a place for living; it was a place for making merry. It had an expansive restau-rant, a lavishly decorated room for after-dinner dancing and a much-used roof garden as well. The Majestic brought to the West Side a clientele whose residential needs could finally justify the inflated prices demanded by the land speculators. Slowly, the sites were purchased and large apartment houses erected on them.

In 1907, the renowned composer Gustav Mahler stayed at the Hotel Majestic for his first season of conducting at the Metropolitan Opera House. And 1907 also saw the erection of the Prasada, at West 65th Street and Central Park West, a few blocks south of Mahler's temporary home *(Figure 61)*.

The Prásáda, to give it its fully accented name, was

Figure 62. *The barrel-vaulted Palm Room of the Prasada in a sketch used for advertising in 1908. (Collection of Andrew Alpern.)*

built by Franklin and Samuel Haines. It was designed by architects Charles W. Romeyn and Henry R. Wynne. Romeyn, the more prominent of the two, was born in 1854 and received his early architectural training in the office of Calvert Vaux, one of the designers of Central Park. He prepared plans for commercial and industrial buildings, later specializing in apartment houses and private residences.

For the Prasada, which carries the address of 50 Central Park West, Romeyn and Wynne selected the French Second Empire style as a base from which to work. Given the origins of the French flats of New York, this was logical, but what these two architects did with that style was rather un-French, and heavy-handed at best.

There is a dry moat surrounding the building and separating it from the pavement. Rising out of this sunken area is a two-story stone base surmounted by an elaborate frieze. At the center of the Central Park West side of the building, four massive banded columns flank the entrance steps and rise double height to support an entablature whose central cartouche proclaims the name of the building.

Beginning at the third floor and going up, the façade presents stiffly academic interpretations of classical French detailing in inelegant combinations. Rusticated stonework at the third floor gives way to stone-balustraded balconies on the fourth. The upper floors offer pseudo-French casement windows with vestigial iron balcony railings, pressed-steel spandrels and a cornice supported on voluted and floriated consoles. Above the cornice are two more stories. Originally there was an elaborately detailed mansard roof embellished with ornamental crestings that concealed the top-floor apartments.

Inside, the Prasada was also lavishly designed, but with a defter touch than on the outside. The entrance steps lead to a semicircular loggia off of which open two maisonettes, later converted to professional offices. At the center axis of the loggia are the entrance doors to the building, which open onto a succession of spaces culminating in a spectacular Palm Room *(Figure 62).*

This waiting space and visual enhancement was designed with a barrel-vaulted, leaded-glass skylight roof supported by four huge carved classical caryatids.

It also boasted an elegant stone fountain backlighted by a wall of leaded stained-glass windows. With the marble benches, the potted palms and the immense oriental rug, the Prasada's Palm Room was a rival of the public spaces of the finest of New York's hotels, albeit on a smaller scale.

Upstairs, each floor originally featured only three apartments. Some subdivisions have since been made, but most remain essentially as they were then. Each rear apartment consists of eight rooms, while each of the two in front has ten. These are spacious, but it is typical of the general attitudes of the time that bathrooms were few. In each case there is a servants' bathroom, but in only one apartment is there more than a single master bath to serve as many as four bedrooms. All the apartments have the dining rooms, libraries and parlors aligned, with sliding pocket doors between, so that extended spaces for entertaining can be created, as large as 15 feet wide by 47 feet long.

According to the original promotional material, special care was taken with the construction of the building and the decoration of the apartment suites. The structure rests on 64 concrete piers, some as large as eight feet square, all running as deep as 40 feet into the ground and resting on solid rock. The upper-floor columns are of rolled steel rather than the often-used cast iron. Cast iron was also rejected for use as plumbing waste lines, galvanized wrought iron being employed instead. An electrical generating plant was located in the basement, with baseboard receptacles provided in the principal rooms and even in some of the bedrooms. There was a mail chute on each floor, a

Figure 63. *The Prasada as it appeared following the 1919 alteration of its top floor. (Joseph Byron, courtesy of the Museum of the City of New York.)*

telephone connection in each apartment, and a central refrigeration plant operated to create ice in the glass- and tile-lined refrigerators in each kitchen.

Parquet wood flooring was laid down in the halls and entertaining rooms of the apartments, with oak paneling in the dining rooms and Caen-stone-mantled gas log fireplaces in those rooms and in the parlors.

All this was to be had at rentals of $300 per month for the largest units. These were impressively large figures for the time, since the financial panic of 1907 had just thrown the entire country into economic chaos. Nonetheless, the apartments rented, tenants moved in and the completed building was occupied as the architects and developers had intended.

In 1919 the mansard-roofed "hat" of the Prasada was replaced with a simple extension of the outside walls of the structure, the new conventional roof hidden by the brick parapet *(Figure 63)*. This alteration gave each apartment on the top floor a few feet more of perimeter space, but the aesthetic damage to the uppermost part of the building is considerable.

A clue to the reason for this curious alteration may be found in a story in the December 15, 1918 edition of the *New York Times*. It was reported that $1,350,000 was to be spent on the Prasada by Penrhyn Stanlaws and Walter Russell. These two had developed several studio apartment houses on nearby West 67th Street, and Walter Russell was in the final stages of complet- ing the Hotel des Artistes on that block. Stanlaws and Russell announced plans to reconstruct the Prasada into a new type of residence—"a combination of club, hotel, and apartment house to meet modern condi- tions."

The concept was to give tenants service, recreation and entertainment in addition to a place to live. Plans called for "tea rooms, dining rooms, and grill rooms" on the first floor. The basement was to contain a marble-and-tile swimming pool, shower baths and a gymnasium. The central kitchen was to serve the public dining facilities as well as providing meals directly to the apartments as requested. It all sounded very similar to the facilities at the Hotel des Artistes.

When all these changes were complete (as designed by architects Starrett and Van Vleck) the apartments were to be sold as cooperatives. Why the scheme was never brought to fruition has not yet been discovered. Only the disfiguring top-floor façade change was made, and many more years were to pass before the rental building was converted to cooperative owner- ship.

As a co-op, however, the Prasada was well main- tained, and an extensive restoration was completed in 1988. With its vigorously detailed façade and unusual entrance loggia, the building is a distinguished survivor in a neighborhood saddled with many newer structures of dubious design.

Hudson on the Hudson

The Hendrik Hudson at 380 Riverside Drive

ON 24 MARCH 1900, at one o'clock in the afternoon, ground was broken in City Hall Park by Mayor Robert A. Van Wyck for New York's first real rapid-transit subway. To be sure, in 1870 Alfred Ely Beach had completed a short experimental subway that ran under Broadway from Warren Street to Murray Street, propelled by a giant fan. At that same point in the city's history, the unsightly elevated railways began to be erected along several routes within Manhattan. But it was the venture of August Belmont, later known as the IRT (Interborough Rapid Transit), that proved to be the most practical.

The Ninth Avenue elevated trains had brought development to the West Side, but the topography of Morningside Heights forced them to veer off to the east at West 110th Street and continue up Eighth Avenue. This left the upper reaches of Riverside Drive and Broadway devoid of public transportation that could even remotely be considered "rapid," effectively isolating the area. With the coming of the new underground transport, however, that isolation was to end.

The prospect of a speedy means of travel to downtown offices, stores and entertainment centers signaled a rise in land prices in the areas that were to be served by the new subway line. Along with those property values, buildings also went up. Novice and seasoned builders alike planned developments, usually apartment houses designed to cater to the newly emerging middle class.

In 1902, two years before the new subway was completed and put into operation, George F. Johnson, Jr. and Aleck Kahn formed a company to erect large apartment houses. Their first project was the Chatsworth, an immense structure at West 72nd Street and Riverside Drive. It was completed just weeks before the subway opened.

The Chatsworth was actually two separate 12-story structures with a common entrance and lobby. These dual buildings contained apartments ranging from a one-bedroom unit (with a dining room and quarters for a servant) to a 15-room unit with 4½ baths. A brisk pace of renting prompted the immediate erection of an adjoining annex, which comprised a single 11-room apartment on each of the seven floors above its lobby level *(Figure 64)*.

Flushed with the success (and cash flow) of the Chatsworth and its annex, and encouraged by the instantaneous acceptance of the new subway by the riding public, developers Johnson and Kahn expanded their operation. They recognized the importance of ready access to the underground trains, and of the proximity of the greenery and fresh air of a park. Moving north from West 72nd Street along the subway line, they stopped at 110th Street (which was also called Cathedral Parkway, since the Cathedral of St. John the Divine was originally planned with its entrance directly on West 110th Street).

At West 110th Street and Broadway, there was the new subway; there were trolley cars; there were the glorious double-decked busses of the Fifth Avenue Coach Company; there was local shopping; and there was Riverside Park only a short block away. Obviously it was an excellent location for an investment by Johnson and Kahn. And invest they did.

They acquired about three-quarters of the block

Above: Figure 64. *The Chatsworth of 1904, 346 West 72nd Street, with the lower limestone annex of the following year adjoining. (Irving Underhill, courtesy of the Museum of the City of New York.)* Opposite, top: Figure 65. *The Hendrik Hudson under construction on March 21, 1907. (Wurts Brothers, courtesy of the Museum of the City of New York.)* Opposite, bottom: Figure 66. *The first section of the Hendrik Hudson at 380 Riverside Drive, with the rooftop arbor in place, 1907. (Wurts Brothers, courtesy of the Museum of the City of New York.)*

defined by upper Riverside Drive, Broadway, and West 110th and 111th Streets. The area was almost vacant, containing only six tiny buildings, four of them wood-framed cottages. Johnson and Kahn then hired the architectural firm of Rouse and Sloan to design an apartment building for the western end of the site, overlooking Riverside Park and elevated well above the river and lower Riverside Drive *(Figure 65)*.

Brilliant and tempestuous young William Lawrence Rouse directed the effort, producing a design modeled on an imaginary grand Tuscan villa. In plan, the building presents a massive solid frontage along Riverside Drive, with deeply recessed "light" courts interrupting the façades fronting on West 110th and 111th Streets. To mark the bend in Riverside Drive not far from the northern end of the building, Rouse proposed a square tower to rise well above the roof line, with a balancing tower a similar distance from the southern street end.

Each of these towers was a spectacular tour-de-force, with open Palladian arches on all four sides, balustraded balconies and decorative terra-cotta panels. Connecting the two towers was a balustraded promenade, which for a brief time was surmounted by an open trelliswork arbor *(Figure 66)*. At the base of each tower, where it joined the main body of the building, a pseudo-Palladian window was originally planned. What was actually built, however, was even more grandiose: an elliptical *œil-de-bœuf* window with cartouche above, carved ornamentation around and swagged garlands flanking.

The towers and the street façades of the building were topped with massive Spanish tile roofs that had extended projections supported on huge bronze brackets. Adding to this grandeur (or overwhelming ostentation, depending on your point of view) were projecting balconies of stone and bronze, scrolled keystones over each window, spherical chimney pots,

Figure 67. *The Hendrik Hudson overlooking the Hudson Fulton celebration of 1909. (Courtesy of the Museum of the City of New York.)*

more cartouches and more garlands. The original plans even called for an elaborately patterned sidewalk pavement, but this element was never constructed.

The building has a classical elegance befitting its prominent position high above Riverside Park. Surrounded by a railed dry moat, there is a two-story rusticated limestone base incorporating arched windows that are detailed to appear as if they were double height. Above the base is Roman brick, laid in a Flemish-bond pattern. The joints are an unusually wide half-inch, deeply raked out to provide shadow lines and an exceptionally rich texture. The upper ornamentation is terra-cotta, lavishly distributed, especially at the uppermost reaches of the building.

George Johnson and Aleck Kahn named the new venture the Hendrik Hudson, appropriately enough considering its location overlooking the Hudson River. It was also, perhaps, a clever marketing ploy anticipating the 1909 Hudson Fulton Celebration, which would commemorate the hundredth anniversary of Robert Fulton's steamboat and the three-hundredth anniversary of Henry Hudson's discovery of Manhattan *(Figure 67)*.

As with the apartment-house ventures of today, the name was important, but so was the lobby design. Basically Italian Renaissance in character, the lobby was marble, with a coffered ceiling, bronze torchères, stone benches and tables, carpeted stairs, potted plants and a huge oriental rug. In attendance were smartly uniformed hall boys and doormen *(Figure 68)*.

The care that went into the design of the building's lobby was extended to the upstairs public corridors. Facing the elevators on the upper floors were windows giving out onto a central courtyard, bringing daylight to what in other buildings of the time was usually a drab interior space. The corridors leading to the apartments were paved in Welsh quarry tiles and were finished in imitation Caen stone. Also contributing natural light, these hallways ended in windows overlooking Riverside Park.

The apartments themselves were unusually well planned for the period, and demonstrated the exceptional skill of William Rouse in residential layout. These abilities were developed and honed in his later partnership with Lafayette A. Goldstone. Under the firm name of Rouse and Goldstone, dozens of well-designed apartment houses were produced. Located on Riverside Drive, Park Avenue, Fifth Avenue and the more fashionable side streets, these developments were presaged by the thoughtful apartment layouts of the Hendrik Hudson.

William Rouse was one of only a handful of architects at the beginning of the twentieth century who were innovative in their handling of the internal arrangements of apartment units designed for the middle class. (Bear in mind that the needs of these families extended to four bedrooms and a library, as well as the customary parlor and a dining room. The key difference revealing the more "modest" clientele was that only a single servant's room would be required.)

Rouse provided a separate service entrance to each apartment, thus keeping the ubiquitous delivery boys away from the family quarters. But even more important, he utilized a central-foyer arrangement. This put the "public" spaces of each apartment nearer the entry and preserved the privacy of the bedrooms, which were reached via a hallway leading off the entrance foyer. Many of the bedrooms could therefore have corner locations, which improved the ventilation in those pre–air-conditioning days. It also obviated the need for the more common long internal hallways that served as circulation spines within the apartments of the period.

As was customary, the dining rooms were often larger than the parlors *(Figure 69)*. Those eating spaces also functioned as the everyday "living" rooms for the families, the parlors being reserved for the formal entertaining of visitors. (The pastor was offered tea in the parlor, but the family would have to make do sitting at the dining-room table.)

Walnut paneling, wood-beamed ceilings, mahogany doors with glass knobs, and the latest designs in porcelain bathroom fittings were all used to attract tenants. Also offered was a billiard parlor, a café, a barber shop and a ladies' hairdressing salon—all for the exclusive use of the building's occupants and guests. Rents ranged from $1500 to $3000 per year *(Figure 70)*.

The Hendrik Hudson at 380 Riverside Drive opened on October 1, 1907. Despite the financial panic that year, it rented unusually rapidly. In a replay of the Chatsworth scenario of three years earlier, even before it was fully occupied, an annex was under construction, completing the West 110th Street frontage and encompassing the Broadway corner *(Figure 71)*.

Carrying the address of 601 West 110th Street, the annex rose 12 stories (the first section had only eight floors). Curiously, although the annex was structurally completely separate from the Riverside Drive building, the apartments on each of its floors continued the lettering designations of the corresponding floors of the earlier structure. Thus, 601 West 110th Street had no apartment 6A, 4B or 8E, for example.

William Rouse also designed the annex, whose elaborate exterior decoration showed a continuity with the earlier building. The water-borne theme of the Hudson Fulton Celebration was reflected in the carved ships' prows (or rostra) used as ornaments high on the façade.

Above, top: Figure 68. *The lobby of 380 Riverside Drive when it was new, 1908. (Collection of Andrew Alpern.)* Above, middle: Figure 69. *A publicity photograph of a dining room at the Hendrik Hudson, 1908. (Collection of Andrew Alpern.)* Above, bottom: Figure 70. *Tenants typically added all the "proper" accoutrements of middle-class decorating tastes, as seen in a photograph of 1910. (Collection of Andrew Alpern.)*

Figure 71. *The completed Hendrik Hudson complex, 1910, with the taller annex to the east, at the Broadway corner. (Irving Underhill, courtesy of the Museum of the City of New York.)*

The Hendrik Hudson and its annex provided substantial and elegant accommodations for those who had the means to enjoy comfortable and spacious apartments. It continued to do this even through the bleak period of the Great Depression. The rent-control law of 1943 limited the profits of landlords, who nevertheless maintained their buildings in their prewar form. This law encouraged the conversion of grand old apartments into multiple units, the subdivisions being done as cheaply as possible. Forty years after they were built, the dual structures designed by William Rouse met that ignominious fate. Subjected to overcrowding and further subdivision into single-room occupancies, the Hendrik Hudson deteriorated rapidly.

The grisly death of a young boy living in the building, who was crushed by one of the elevators, brought a public outcry. The resultant investigation

and ownership change brought about a renovation in 1959. While far from anything even approaching a restoration of what once was, small apartments that were at least decent and habitable were created. In the process, however, much of what produced the distinction of the façade was removed.

In 1970, the Hendrik Hudson was converted to cooperative ownership. Original offering prices ranged from $4800 for a first-floor studio to $26,100 for a top-floor three-bedroom unit with a river view (and a monthly maintenance of $315). What the purchasers received was far from what William Rouse had designed 60 years earlier. On the other hand, in retrospect, the subsequent capital appreciation in the value of those apartments made them an excellent investment. But for the rent-control laws, however, it might have been the *original* apartments that were for sale in 1970. Now *those* would have been investments!

Regal Riverside

*Continental grandeur overlooking the river
at 404 Riverside Drive*

IN 1865, WORK ON the construction of Central Park was well under way, and enthusiasm for civic improvements had been rekindled by the ending of the Civil War. That year, a modest pamphlet was published by William R. Martin. It suggested that the escarpments along the projected northern route of Twelfth Avenue above West 72nd Street might be better utilized as an ornamental park. The following year, a bill was introduced in the state legislature to create the proposed improvement. Written and promoted by the protean champion of the city's development, Andrew Haswell Green, the bill became law on April 24, 1867. That was the birth date of Riverside Park.

The area was certainly appropriate to a facility that could make readily available to the general public the splendors of the Hudson River and the majestic views of the Palisades beyond. Until that time, the riverfront had been reserved for those whose property abutted the water. Houses, most of wood-frame construction, had been built earlier all along the riverbank. Some were modest *(Figure 72)*, others were quite grand *(Figure 73)*.

By the time all the land for the park had been acquired in 1872 (at a cost of more than $6 million), Frederick Law Olmsted had completed his designs for the project. Olmsted's scheme was a sensitive naturalistic adaptation of English park theory to the exceedingly linear property he had to work with. Departing from the straight-edged plan of Central Park, the eastern border of Riverside Park followed the existing undulating crest of the embankment and was defined by the new Riverside Drive.

Conceived of as a grand European-style boulevard, the drive was envisioned as forming the city's preeminent residential street, expected to eclipse Fifth Avenue with ease. To provide yet greater grandeur and privacy for the elegant mansions that were expected, an even more twisting and much narrower upper service road was planned for the stretch from West 97th to 113th Street, separated from the lower roadway by a thickly planted and sloping minipark that might serve as a visual "front yard" for the anticipated estates.

With the opening of the park and the drive in 1880 (following pitched battles between local residents and an allegedly unpaid contractor), development of the adjoining building lots began in earnest. The northern corner of West 114th Street had earlier seen the erection of the grandly Corinthian-columned Carrington Rudd mansion *(Figure 74)* and its splendid siting was emulated on the block directly to the south for the rambling three-story granite pile constructed for George Noakes *(Figure 75)*.

Further down the drive other grand houses were built, including the spectacular full-block château of steel magnate Charles M. Schwab *(Figure 76)*. This was lost to the city when Mayor Fiorello La Guardia refused to accept it as a mayoral residence, allegedly because its lavishness, 75 rooms and grand scale made him feel even smaller than he already was *(Figure 77)*. Of all these monuments to conspicuous consumption and expansive living, the only ones remaining are the landmarked Isaac Rice mansion at West 89th Street (now a school but originally built as a home for an

Above, top: Figure 72. *A simple frame house overlooking the Hudson. The view, ca. 1890, is west from 11th Avenue (later renamed West End Avenue) with West 94th Street newly cut through. (Courtesy of the Museum of the City of New York.)* Above, bottom: Figure 73. *The house of William P. Furniss, its grounds occupying the entire block bounded by Riverside Drive, West End Avenue, West 99th Street and 100th Street. It was taken down in 1904. (Robert L. Bracklow, courtesy of The New-York Historical Society.)*

Above, top: Figure 74. *The mid-nineteenth-century Carrington Rudd mansion at the north corner of West 114th Street and Riverside Drive, ca. 1905. (Courtesy of the Museum of the City of New York.)* Above, bottom: Figure 75. *The deceptively permanent-looking stone mansion of George Noakes, designed by Arthur B. Jennings, on Riverside Drive between West 113th and 114th Streets. It stood only from 1884 to 1906. (George William Sheldon.)*

Above: Figure 76. *The château of Charles Schwab at West 73rd Street and Riverside Drive in 1906, a week before Schwab moved in.* (*Eugene Wemlinger, courtesy of the Museum of the City of New York.*) Opposite: Figure 77. *A portion of the west terrace of the Schwab mansion in 1916.* (*Courtesy of the Museum of the City of New York.*)

industrialist whose wife was the founder of the Society for the Suppression of Unnecessary Noise) and the similarly protected Morris Schinasi house on West 107th Street, later used as a school and now reconverted to residential use *(Figure 78).*

Complementing the private houses, a number of fine apartment houses had been built along the section of the drive south of West 110th Street, but the area to the north was especially slow to develop, no doubt because convenient rapid-transit facilities were few. Indeed, more than half the available building sites along the entire drive were still vacant in 1902.

All this was changed dramatically with the opening of the Broadway subway line in 1904. As soon as the

construction work on the project had begun in 1900, land prices rose precipitously, as did apartment houses for those with modest incomes and for richer people as well. Even before the vacant sites had been filled in, almost-new mansions were razed to make way for the more profitable multiple dwellings. The George Noakes house, only 22 years old, was taken down in 1906 to allow for the erection of the Riverside Mansions at 410 Riverside Drive. The Carrington Rudd place fell victim to the wrecker's hammer a few years later so that 420 Riverside Drive, the Hamilton, could replace it.

Following the trend toward large apartment houses was the Strathmore, at 404 Riverside Drive *(Figure*

Figure 78. *The Morris Schinasi residence at West 107th Street and Riverside Drive, completed in 1909 to designs of William B. Tuthill. (Irving Underhill, courtesy of the Museum of the City of New York.)*

79). Located on the southern corner of West 113th Street, the site had been bought in 1887 by William Waldorf Astor and might have been used for his planned new mansion had he not changed his mind and built instead on Fifth Avenue. Designed by the prolific architectural firm of Schwartz & Gross, whose specialty was apartment houses, Number 404 stood out from the rest by the exceptionally fine quality of its design and its construction. Filed with the Department of Buildings in 1908 for the Akron Building Company at an estimated cost of $300,000, the 12-story building showed a classical façade in the tradition of the École des Beaux-Arts. Echoing the form of Greek and Roman columns, there is a base of crisply articulated limestone, a shaft of dark red brick, and a

multistory capital of limestone and terra-cotta, with a massive metal cornice crowned with sentinel-like antefixes (anthemia of an architectural past).

Of particular interest and elegance is the entrance *(Figure 80)*. Avoiding the pseudo-monumentality (and impracticality) of a flight of steps, the architect achieved grandeur at a residential scale through the use of curving granite cheek walls, majestic multi-armed torchères and a splendid and gracefully curved iron-and-glass marquee. Requiring vigilant maintenance to prevent their rusting away, glazed iron canopies have become a rarity in New York, but are a familiar sight along the boulevards of Europe and South America. In 1983, this imagery prompted the exterior of 404 Riverside Drive to be used (with temporarily replaced street signs) to represent a dwelling on a fashionable *avenida* in Buenos Aires for the television film *Prisoner Without a Name, Cell Without a Number.*

The interior shots for the movie were made in an apartment on Park Avenue, but not for want of lavish accommodations at Number 404. Inside, the architect had divided each floor into two 10-room apartments of about 3500 square feet apiece. Enjoying exceptionally high ceilings, complex plasterwork moldings, walnut paneling and elaborately bordered parquet floors, the primary rooms of each unit were planned *en suite* and commanded expansive views of Riverside Park, the Hudson River and the Palisades beyond. Original rents ranged from $2500 to an expensive $3900 a year.

Schwartz & Gross, founded in 1902 by Simon Schwartz and Arthur Gross, both then 25 years old, has sometimes been looked upon as a hack firm, turning out plans for scores of mediocre apartment houses over an extended period of time. But when given an enlightened client and a sufficient budget, the firm was quite capable of producing buildings that might cater to a tenancy with more than the usual needs and taste.

They demonstrated this at 404, where the apartments have mahogany doors, crystal doorknobs, leaded decorative-glass transoms, bathtubs sized for couples and circular stall showers formed by a cage of chromed water pipes that can attack a weary body from every conceivable position and angle.

Completed in 1909 and catering to tenants whose names could be found in the various published lists of socially well-established and active New Yorkers, the building had a succession of owners, all of whom gave exceptional attention to maintaining both the fabric and the amenities of the building. Economic realities of the 1930s, of course, took their toll, many of the apartments being subdivided into two, or even three, smaller units whose rents were more accessible to New Yorkers straitened by the Depression. Although there are now double the number of suites that existed in 1909, a surprising number of the original apartments still exist, including the building's only duplex, which connects a portion of the lobby floor to the apartment above.

After 1922, ownership of the building was in the hands of longtime city official and activist Newbold Morris, who continued his family's venerable tradition of promoting city living at its best by running the building in a manner approaching that of a philanthropy. Following his instructions, the building was offered to its tenantry after he died. In what must have set an all-time record for speed in such matters, title was taken by the tenants' cooperative corporation on June 30, 1967, less than a year after the concept was first proposed.

The change in ownership status was barely noticed in the day-to-day affairs of the building, so well had it been run before. There was certainly never any thought given to replacing any of the employees. Indeed, an indication of their loyalty was evidenced by the request of Eddie Butler on his deathbed that he be buried in the doorman's uniform he had worn so proudly for more than 20 years.

Loyalty toward the Strathmore is not confined just to those who serve the tenants but extends to the

Figure 79. *The Strathmore, by architects Schwartz & Gross, at 404 Riverside Drive, ca. 1910. (Irving Underhill, courtesy of the Museum of the City of New York.)*

tenants themselves. There is an apartment on the tenth floor (still in its original 10-room form) which has had only two resident families since it was built. The first was the Simons, whose ownership of Carnegie Hall for many years maintained it for Isaac Stern's eventual preservation triumph. Ultimately, the Simon daughter married the son of the Simon housekeeper, which caused a bit of a social stir before it was realized that they made a charming and gracious couple.

Equally loyal were longterm residents Frank Hogan,

Manhattan's longtime district attorney, and teacher-philosopher Reinhold Niebuhr. Proof of how strong an attachment can be engendered in the building is given by a blind young social worker who lived there with his wife and child. He left to start a new life in Florida, but when he found that, for him, rural living was not compatible with blindness, he returned to the city. He would not settle in permanently, however, until he was again able to obtain an apartment at the Strathmore.

Figure 80. *The entrance to 404 Riverside Drive in 1982, with its cast-iron torchères, wrought-iron scroll brackets and a marquee that originally was glazed. (Andrew Alpern.)*

Eclectic Elegance

Hard-fought survival and rebirth at
45 East 66th Street

NEW YORK APARTMENT HOUSES can be found in all sizes and shapes. Architecturally, they can readily be separated into several reasonably discrete categories that parallel their chronology. Thus we have today's highly stylized offerings, easily distinguished from the bland brick boxes of the 1960s and 1970s, which are in turn clearly different from the more Classically inspired constructions of the 1920s and 1930s.

Among the thousands of multiple dwellings in New York, few stand out as being particularly unusual; few demonstrate the sort of eccentric or eclectic elegance that is more often encountered in one-family residential buildings. Since practically all New York apartment houses have been erected on speculation by builders seeking a profit from their investment, it is really not surprising that conservative restraint has generally been favored as an architectural imperative over a freer, more eclectic use of historical precedent.

A notable exception is 45 East 66th Street, which stands out as curiously non–New York in feeling *(Figure 81)*. Each city has its own "feel": the corners of most buildings in Copenhagen are chamfered (to permit fire apparatus to negotiate turns along the narrow streets); the façades of structures in London have Classical detailing on a domestic scale; while the architectural decoration in Paris tends to be florid, overblown and grandiose. By contrast, pre–World War II apartment buildings in New York were most often designed with ornamented tops and bottoms, but with relatively plain mid-sections—rather like Greek or Roman columns. Not so 45 East 66th Street, where the street fronts of the entire building are given ornate and elaborate articulation.

The immediate prominence of number 45 is the full-height 180-degree rounded corner tower. Towers and turrets are of course common to churches, and are occasionally seen on private houses, but they are rare on conventional apartment houses. Even more rare is the use of sixteenth-century Elizabethan multipaned glazing, and a façade encrusted with pseudo-Gothic detailing. But the most improbable feature of 45 East 66th Street is the multifeatured top of the structure. Above the uppermost row of windows is a series of filigreed arches, each with crockets up the sides and culminating in a finial. These are set against a brick wall topped with a bracketed round-arch arcade, surmounted in turn by a large projecting cornice. Originally, the cornice was crowned with an open demicolonnaded parapet, which made the highest point on the façade a full two stories above the building's top floor. (The parapet balustrade deteriorated from exposure to the weather and had to be removed many years ago.) The upper portion of the façade still tends to look like a stage set when viewed from the north, however. The extension of the building's face well above the roof can be readily seen, along the angled steel beams needed to support it.

The elevations of the building show an intricate complexity of surface treatment and a flamboyance that has few equals in all of the city. The articulation of the façade is accentuated when the sun brings out the shadows formed by the multiple levels of the surface, with the two-color scheme of red brick and tan terracotta contributing the final measure of complexity.

The architect of 45 East 66th Street was the firm of Harde & Short. Herbert Harde used the technique of

the rounded full-height corner tower in his earlier seven-story apartment houses at the northwest corner of West 80th Street and West End Avenue. The real antecedent for 45 East, however, was Harde & Short's Red House at 350 West 85th Street. This six-story side-street building shows the same brick-and-terracotta color scheme, the large expanses of multipane windows, the strong vertical piers and the Gothic-inspired hood encrustations over some of the window enframements. The stylistic origins of 45 East 66th have been traced even further back. Precedents can be seen in the Gothic civil architecture of fifteenth- and sixteenth-century Belgium: the incredibly gingerbread Town Hall at Louvain, erected circa 1450, and the House of the Guild of Masons at Ghent from the following century.

In addition to the Flemish historical models for 45 East 66th Street, Elizabethan design approaches and French styles influenced Harde & Short. This extreme eclecticism was compounded by the huge size of the structure when compared to the modest brownstones that originally surrounded it. To say the least, the building was arresting.

Also dramatic was the original floor plan. A typical floor comprised only two apartments. The public areas of each included a room-sized windowed foyer, a music room, a dining room (plus a small conservatory), a living room and a large salon, all totaling about 1600 square feet. There were three or four bedrooms, provision for household help, and an additional bedroom for a personal lady's maid. Closet space was ample, and each suite had four bathrooms.

Plans for this magnificent structure were filed with the city in May 1906 and the building was suitably dubbed the Parkview, reflecting the view that early upper-floor tenants could enjoy. That name faded into the woodwork, however, after the initial renting season. Despite the financial panic of 1907, the apartments rented well, but neighborhood change had its effect on the building. The post-1910 heavy development of Fifth and Park Avenues with apartment houses dictated the alteration of much of the street-level space along Madison Avenue to commercial uses. To accommodate this, the owners of 45 East 66th Street gradually removed the protective iron railing, filled in the moat surrounding the building and converted the ground floor to stores.

By 1929, Madison Avenue stores commanded sufficiently high rentals to prompt a major alteration of the building's ground floor. Until that time, the structure's entrance was at the corner of the block and the building carried the address of 777 Madison Avenue. Thomas & Churchill, the architects who were hired for the alteration project, relocated the entrance to the easternmost corner, making the corresponding change in the official address. The entire ground-floor space was then consolidated and new shopfronts constructed along the Madison Avenue frontage.

Somewhat surprisingly, the apartments upstairs survived the Depression of the 1930s intact. It was the "temporary" wartime rent-control law that proved architecturally more destructive. It was only by subdividing apartments that an owner could escape the restrictions of the law, so between 1948 and 1953 those apartments that became vacant (whether naturally or through eviction) were cut in two. Although still large by today's standards, these units lack the grandeur of the originals. Several untouched single suites remain, but it is only the tenth floor that is in its virgin two-families-per-floor condition.

The building is certainly not in the same state it was when the Wurts Brothers took photographs of it early in the twentieth century. But it has been well preserved and restored, doubtless thanks in large measure to the strenuous activities of its tenantry, which organized and fought whenever necessary.

Sold by the Bing & Bing organization to horseman–real-estate mogul Sigmund Sommer in 1973, the building experienced a change in services. Threatened with conversion of the elevators to automatic operation, the tenants brought a lawsuit. The case was resolved at the appeals level with a $2500 fine for Sommer and an assurance of continued manual operation of the elevators for the tenants. The strength of the tenants' group apparently was more than Sommer could handle, since he sold the building back to Bing & Bing only two months later.

In 1977 the tenants again joined together to lobby to have their home designated by the New York City Landmarks Preservation Commission, and, bolstered by professional research and advocacy, succeeded in their quest for official landmarking. Residents rallied once more when a cooperative conversion plan was presented, and they negotiated as a group, thus benefiting their own common interests. By working cooperatively, the occupants of 45 East 66th Street ensured that their distinctive home would be well maintained and would flourish . . . to their personal financial benefit, and to the delight and pleasure of all pedestrians who can look at the building and enjoy this monument to eclectic elegance.

Opposite: Figure 81. *45 East 66th Street when it was new and known as 777 Madison Avenue. (Wurts Brothers, courtesy of the Museum of the City of New York.)*

Resurrection Redux

Alwyn Court is twice reborn at 180 West 58th Street

THE PHŒNIX WAS A legendary bird that periodically rose from the ashes of its own funeral pyre to live again. By that standard, Alwyn Court ought to be renamed the Phœnix. Twice in its relatively brief lifetime of well under a century, the building has been reborn. It is now a splendid and elegant cooperative whose need for future rebirths would appear to be a long way off.

Alwyn Court was built at 180 West 58th Street, on the corner of Seventh Avenue, across from the grandiose grotesquerie of the Navarro's eight-building complex and just a block from Central Park. It was named for Alwyn Ball, Jr., a director of Heddon Construction Company, the builder-developer of the venture. Designed by the architects Herbert Spencer Harde and R. Thomas Short, Alwyn Court is a 12-story confection encrusted with repetitive white terracotta ornament in the Francis I style of the early French Renaissance *(Figure 82)*.

The accommodations provided to tenants of Alwyn Court were exceedingly lavish—not surprisingly, since annual rentals ran from $6500 to $10,000 for the standard apartments, up to $22,000 a year for one special duplex unit. Considering that one could live quite decently at the time on an income of less than $2000 per year, these were astounding rentals.

But what one got for the money was equally impressive. The suites ranged in size from 14 to 34 rooms, with extra-large spaces and extra-high ceilings. The "public" rooms of one of the standard apartments were comprised of a gallery, a reception room, a salon, a "music room," a living room, a library, a conservatory and a dining room. These were cleverly arranged so they could be thrown together into a continuous suite for entertaining that encompassed about 2500 square feet—the total size of an ordinary brownstone row house.

The fitments and decorations were described in the *Real Estate Record and Guide* shortly after the building had opened:

> That chamber [at the corner of the building] is a grand room for the prospect it gives out over the Plaza and Central Park, and also for its own interior finish of white enamel woodwork and silken hangings. Back of it is my lady's dressing-room, where every panel is a mirror, and every mirror hides a closet in the wall. A singular thing about the doors in this room and in some others is that they have no visible hinges and locks; and one who did not know would see no door at all, as doors have the appearance of panels merely. The walls and ceilings of the bathrooms and dressing-rooms are mirrored also. The shelves in all the bathrooms and dressing-rooms are plate glass. There are roomy millinery closets with plate glass compartments, fireplaces of exquisite design, parquet floors, mahogany doors, paneled walls in the dining rooms, and woodwork elsewhere in white with "compo" ornamentation in floral designs.

With such similarly grand apartment houses as the Osborne across the avenue, and with Carnegie Hall a block away, Alwyn Court flourished. Changing whims of fashion, however, and, more drastically, the changing fortunes of the Depression era, put impossible pressures on the building. The market for huge apartments dried up and the building's no-longer-

Figure 82. *Alwyn Court in 1908, with the rental sign still fixed to the side offering "Suites of 14 rooms and 5 bathrooms" to "Suites of 34 rooms and 9 bathrooms. Rental of $6,500 and upward." "Open for Inspection." (Courtesy of the Museum of the City of New York.)*

fashionable location exacerbated the situation. As leases expired, the apartments were vacated and remained unrentable.

The last tenant left in 1936, and the building was sealed. The Dry Dock Savings Bank had already foreclosed the mortgage, having invested some $900,000 in the property. With taxes running $30,000 per year and no income flowing from the building, drastic measures were needed.

As originally designed, the apartments were based on an elaborate ritual of dining in and entertaining. There was even a separate wine cellar in the basement for each of the units. But in 1936 there was little money available for entertaining lavishly, and dining out had become socially acceptable. Clearly, a major conversion to smaller units was needed.

Although the structure was in splendid physical condition, the arrangement of the walls, the elevators

Above, left: Figure 83. *Alwyn Court in January 1938, its grand apartments vacant and unrentable. (Wurts Brothers, courtesy of the Museum of the City of New York.)* Above, right: Figure 84. *A portion of the north façade of Alwyn Court in October 1938 showing its elaborate ornament and the lions flanking the private entrance to one of the building's maisonette apartments. (Wurts Brothers, courtesy of the Museum of the City of New York.)* Left: Figure 85. *The reconstructed version of Alwyn Court showing the lobotomized top and the crudely closed off corner entrance. The photograph dates to October 1938, just nine months after the alteration work began. (Wurts Brothers, courtesy of the Museum of the City of New York.)*

and the stairs, not to mention new building code requirements, made it impractical to consider any alteration of the interior. A complete reconstruction was the only possibility, and this to a building not even 30 years old *(Figure 83)*.

Edgar Ellinger was a 25-year veteran of the New York building and real-estate industry, with experience in planning, construction, marketing and management. He proposed totally gutting the interior of the building, removing the elevators and stairs, and leaving only the exterior walls, floor arches and steel framework. All the lavish interior detailing was to be demolished, including the replication of a French stone castle that was included within one of the 34-room apartments. Most of the exterior ornament was to remain *(Figure 84)*. The bank accepted the plan.

Using the services of architect Louis Weeks, Ellinger developed a new arrangement for the building that included six apartments to a floor, each of three, four or five rooms, along with new elevators, two firestairs (the old building having had only one) and a public corridor surrounding the interior courtyard on three sides. That corridor was to prove of great value 45 years later.

The architectural planning additionally called for the creation of three new penthouse units on the roof (roofs were considered suitable only for servants when Alwyn Court was constructed), and the building's entrance was relocated close to the southwestern corner to make room for income-producing commercial space. The penthouses called for terraces with views of Central Park, but this required the visually brutalizing removal of the building's magnificently grand and multitiered balustraded cornice *(Figure 85)*. Total cost for the reconstruction of the building: about $500,000, all of which was provided by the Dry Dock Savings Bank.

Ellinger's firm was retained to serve as renting and managing agent. In nine months the building was almost completely rented, with an annual gross cash flow of about $137,000.

All went well for many years, but gradually things deteriorated. Rent-control laws put the building into a precarious financial position and a dramatic change was again needed to restore Alwyn Court to its rightful place among the luxury apartment buildings of the city.

Beyer Blinder Belle is an architectural firm that specializes in restoration projects and in historic landmark structures. In 1982, the firm was retained to consider how the building might best be restored or altered. High on the list was the cleaning and restoration of the elaborately ornamental façade. This was a tedious and complex process, which involved hand-scrubbing with a succession of special chemical solutions, repointing of all joints and recaulking of all windows, as well as recreation of damaged or missing decorative elements.

The ground-floor commercial space was rearranged and a *très grand luxe* restaurant constructed with its entrance at the corner, where the building's original 1908 entrance had been.

Most important, however, was a change to the interior "jail house courtyard" (so dubbed by Dr. James Marston Fitch, an architectural historian and a former Columbia University professor). Something needed to be done.

Figure 86. *The reconstructed central court of Alwyn Court, 1983, showing the trompe-l'œil decoration created by muralist Richard Haas. (Alan Schindler, courtesy of Beyer Blinder Belle.)*

It was. First, the open courtyard was roofed over with a huge insulated glass skylight, turning what had been an outside yard into an inside atrium. Then the windows of the three-sided public corridor on the each floor were removed, and replaced with simple open railings. The ground level of the new atrium was floored with varicolored marbles and furnished with carved stone benches, potted trees and a dramatic multijet fountain. And most important, the entire inside surface of what had once been a plain-brick giant air shaft was repainted by muralist Richard Haas into a trompe-l'œil reinterpretation of the original ornamental decoration from the outside façade of the building *(Figure 86)*.

Alwyn Court began life as a grand residence for 22 families. It became obsolete and was reborn as an apartment house for its time. And now it has again risen from its own ashes, facing the future with renewed vigor and a clean face.

Meandering Montana

Apartment appellations depict a wandering West,
with a settlement at 375 Park Avenue

MONTANA IS ASSUMED TO be out *West* but in New York, Montana was first East and later West. Then it went East again, and most recently it showed up for the fourth time . . . on the Upper *West* Side. And Nebraska, Wyoming, Dakota, Yosemite, Idaho and Indiana were all over the map. Geography would seem to be quite malleable when applied to apartment-house nomenclature.

The first of the four Montanas was built at 155 East 48th Street. It was a five-story, 25-foot wide, brownstone-fronted block of flats: more than a tenement but certainly not luxury digs. Built about 1877, it was the mate to an identical building next door—the Idaho. There were hundreds of similar buildings all over town, each with the indoor plumbing and the windows in every room that were to be mandated in 1901 as the minimum for even a tenement house. By the time the 1901 tenement-house law was passed, however, the old flat buildings like that first Montana were outdated and destined for the wrecker's ball. The death knell came for the Montana-Idaho pair in 1928. They were torn down and replaced with a single six-story elevator apartment house that was more in tune with those "modern" times.

The first Montana memorialized a territory. By the time the second was built around 1900, Montana had become a full-fledged state. Reflecting that new status,

Montana II was higher on the scale of apartment accommodations. Built to six stories on a 100-foot-square corner plot overlooking Mount Morris Park at West 124th Street, the structure boasted an elevator and had apartments as large as ten rooms (renting for $100 per month in 1914). It was clearly middle-class *(Figure 87)*.

By far the most memorable Montana, however, was the one erected in 1913 on the site of what had been the Steinway Piano Factory at Park Avenue from East 52nd to 53rd Street *(Figure 88)*. The developers were the Potter brothers—E. Clifford Potter and Fred G. Potter—who had gotten into the Western swing of things by building the Wyoming on Seventh Avenue a few years earlier. The architects for the new Montana were Rouse and Goldstone, the successor firm to Rouse and Sloan, which had designed the Wyoming. William Lawrence Rouse had formed the new partnership with Lafayette A. Goldstone, who proved to be especially adept at luxury-apartment-house planning.

The exterior design of the new Montana was a modern interpretation of various Italian Renaissance architectural forms but, curiously, it bore a certain vague similarity to the piano factory formerly on the site. The round-arched windows, the flat pilasters, the corbelled cornice arcade and the unusual angled pseudo-pediment at the center of the Park Avenue

Opposite, top: Figure 87. *The second Montana apartment house, at West 124th Street and Mount Morris Park. (Courtesy of the Museum of the City of New York.)* Opposite, bottom: Figure 88. *The Steinway piano factory on Park Avenue before the railway tracks were lowered. (*Leslie's Illustrated Weekly, *September 22, 1860, courtesy of Christopher Gray.)*

Figure 89. *The third and most famous Montana Apartments, at 375 Park Avenue, 1913. (Wurts Brothers, courtesy of the Museum of the City of New York.)*

façade all could be found on both the Steinway structure and the new apartment building *(Figure 89)*. Merely a coincidence?

As with the builders' earlier Wyoming, the avenue entrance of the Montana boasted a grand carriage driveway. It led to a 150-foot-long lobby whose repetitive shallow stone arches were strongly reminiscent of the arcade at the Lexington Avenue entry to Grand Central Terminal *(Figure 90)*. Five passenger elevators (with four additional service cars) gave access to the nine apartments on each of the building's upper 11 floors. Those dwellings were said at the time to be "comparatively small," although the least of them had eight rooms and the largest 12. Two lines of apartments were "duplexed," with a flight of stairs

replacing the usual corridor to the bedroom wing. Thus, the apartments had the feel of a two-story house, although the bedrooms were not directly over the living rooms.

The A-line apartment on each floor had a 650-square-foot living room directly adjoining a 320-square-foot reception room, a 350-square-foot dining room and a 255-square-foot library—a total of 1575 square feet of entertaining space, not counting the four bedrooms, two servants' rooms, servants' dining room, kitchen, pantry and four bathrooms.

The fitments and finishes of these apartments complemented their spatial grandeur. Kitchen stoves had eight burners and included two ovens, a broiler and a plate warmer. Hardware throughout was of bronze, with mahogany doors to all rooms. The painted woodwork was finished with four coats of paint topped with two of enamel. Elaborate stone mantels were provided for the fireplaces supplied to each living room.

The luxury in the public spaces of the Montana were no less than that in the private. At the carriage entrance was temporary parking for three or four "motor cars," with a waiting room for their chauffeurs. Nearby was a shop vending flowers, newspapers and magazines, and an office for the concierge. Accessible from the lobby was a large grillroom for the exclusive use of residents and their guests, with a small separate dining room for their servants. Also serving the premises were a barber shop, a manicure parlor and a minihotel of furnished rooms for the use of the residents' guests.

Fifty extra maids' rooms were provided on the uppermost floor, along with 52 individual laundries. Storage rooms for each tenant were built in the basement and a private telephone system interconnected all these facilities with the apartments.

It has been waggishly said that location represents 120 percent of a building's total value, but the shifting sands of locational imperatives can doom a structure far faster than functional obsolescence. The Montana was erected at 375 Park Avenue as a very long-term investment property. It was designed with the finest of materials—both evident and hidden—and was planned with apartments whose like cannot eco-

Figure 90. *The shallow arches of the Montana's lobby, seen in a photograph of 1916, are reminiscent of the arches of the Lexington Avenue arcade of Grand Central Terminal. (Courtesy of the Museum of the City of New York.)*

Figure 91. *The most recent use of Montana as an apartment-house name is on Broadway and West 87th Street. The patch of repair tape on the almost-new entrance awning is indicative of the quality of the building. (Philip Greenberg.)*

nomically now be duplicated. Nonetheless, when residential usage was pushed out after World War II by the expanding need for midtown office space, the Montana was unceremoniously torn down, and in its place the Seagram Building was erected.

The stretch of Park Avenue between East 57th Street and Grand Central Terminal once housed a procession of grand apartment houses that had space, service, substance and style. They were erected with the expectation that they would last . . . if not forever, at least several lifetimes. They were rental buildings at a time when owning a share in a really fine apartment house was akin to holding a substantial portfolio of the bluest of the blue chips. Nonetheless, all that is left of those apartment houses is fading memories—and 417 Park Avenue.

The elegant and spacious 417 Park is still there because it is a cooperative. It is *home* to its owners, not merely an investment to be exchanged for another if a higher yield can be perceived elsewhere. Had the Montana been built as a cooperative, or converted to one before the war, the building might well be still catering to discerning (and wealthy) tenants. Although the conventional wisdom of investor-owners of rental apartment houses said that intrusive office usage in a neighborhood would reduce the income potential of such properties, resident-owners of cooperative apart-

ment houses would be more likely to recognize the inherent value of living within walking distance of their offices. The owners of 417 Park preserved their building in that way. Would that 375 Park had had a similar opportunity!

Although Number 375 is gone, the name Montana is with us for the fourth time in the form of a modern twin-towered structure at Broadway on the blockfront from West 87th to 88th street *(Figure 91)*. This sad parody of the once-proud title "luxury apartment house" attempts to emulate the Eldorado, the Majestic or the Century on Central Park West, but the exigencies of present-day construction costs make it look far better in the architect's original design rendering than it does in reality. Touted as offering "traditional" spacious family apartments, the new Montana in fact has room sizes and layouts that are no more related to the great West Side apartments of the first quarter of this century than are the present rents ($6600 a *month* for three bedrooms) comparable to the price of $6600 a *year* for which one could lease a high-ceilinged home in the prior Montana . . . and one which contained *three* times as much square footage. Names can be recycled and the rental brochures can pour out the hype, but the financial realities of today have effectively guaranteed that the luxury apartment houses of the past will never be recreated.

Holdout House

The last of its breed at 417 Park Avenue

AS MIDTOWN PARK AVENUE'S grand old apartment houses have given way to offices in recent years, one building has stood against the tide: 417 Park, perhaps the most elegant and skillfully designed of the lot.

It was among the earliest of the luxury apartment houses built in the early 1900s, soon after Park Avenue as we know it was born. The boulevard was previously called Fourth Avenue, but it had always been extra wide north of East 42nd Street to accommodate the railroad tracks, which were first installed in 1834. When the tracks were lowered below grade in the early 1870s, following the construction of Commodore Vanderbilt's first Grand Central Depot, real-estate speculators and developers thought that the avenue's width could be used to advantage. It was not until the electrification of the railway was begun in 1903, however, that the stage was set for the development of Park Avenue proper. With electrified trains, there would be no more smoke and soot, and the sunken tracks could then be completely roofed over with little parks.

The Mayfair Apartments at the southeast corner of East 57th Street and Park Avenue was one of the earliest. Erected in 1904 to the designs of Lamb & Rich, the building was an exuberant concoction of limestone and brick *(Figure 92)*. It featured three apartments on each of its 12 floors, and had four elevators. The units comprised seven or eight rooms, but included only two bathrooms apiece and no

Figure 92. *The original presentation rendering of the 1904 Mayfair Apartments at East 57th Street and Park Avenue. (Courtesy of Christopher Gray and the Museum of the City of New York.)*

Left: Figure 93. *A 1930 view of 410 Park Avenue on the right, with its later imitation at 400 Park at the left. Both have been replaced by office buildings. (Wurts Brothers, courtesy of the Museum of the City of New York.)*

Right: Figure 94. *The elegant and refined 417 Park Avenue, when new in 1916. (Wurts Brothers, courtesy of Christopher Gray and the Museum of the City of New York.)*

bathtubs for the servants. The rooms were not large, but were enhanced by multiple bay windows, which also lent visual interest to the façade. The Mayfair was really a nineteenth-century apartment house—old-fashioned before its time and not what the twentieth century called for. Nonetheless, it survived until 1946, and was considered an elegant place to live by journalist-writer Helen Worden, who lived there with her mother early in the century.

More in tune with the century's "modern" aesthetics was 410 Park, designed by Julius Harder and erected in 1914 at the southwest corner of East 55th Street. It had a restrained, elegant, all-limestone façade and refined Classical detailing. Layouts better met the needs of the rapidly developing upper-income neighborhood south of 57th Street. The lower floors had two apartments apiece of 11 and 13 rooms. Each of the upper floors comprised one grand 18-room apartment. Builder Cauldwell-Wingate's work at 410 Park must have impressed developer S. Fullerton Weaver, who decided to put up a similar structure next door at Number 400 (*Figure 93*). Weaver hired the firm of Warren & Wetmore (fresh from completing the new Grand Central Terminal), which produced a comparable all-limestone, Classically detailed façade and a 12-room and a 13-room apartment on each floor.

Throughout history architects have cloned each other's buildings, and a third example appeared in 1916 at 417 Park Avenue, across the street from the first one.

The new apartment house was the most skillfully designed of the three—not at all surprising considering the significant architectural skills of its creator, Emery Roth. Roth's design was executed on commission from the developers Leo and Alexander Bing, and resulted in an ultra-elegant and superbly proportioned building (*Figure 94*). Its careful restraint and almost academic perfection are far more akin to the work of Charles Follen McKim (exemplified by the reserved 998 Fifth Avenue of only a few years earlier) than to the major corpus of Roth's work—both before and after this project.

Although 417 Park Avenue was an anomaly, it was one that proved Roth was capable of switching styles with ease. Setting aside his customary bold and lusty design features, Roth treated 417 with delicate restraint. He subdivided and embellished the smooth limestone façade with continuous belt courses, balconies, colonnettes, pediments and decorative cartouches, all understated. The discreet side-street entrance originally lacked so much as an awning, and the modest pediment and supporting console brackets contrasted strongly with the vigor of Roth's other apartment-house entries. His virtuosity came to the fore, nonetheless, in the building's complexly detailed and deeply cantilevered copper cornice.

The lower floors of the building were designed with two apartments apiece of eight and 11 rooms; the upper four floors each originally housed a single 16-room apartment. To assure better light and air to the apartments, the developer purchased an adjoining 25-foot-wide lot and built a two-story garage (with chauffeurs' rooms on the upper floor), sympathetically designed in Classically detailed limestone by the architectural firm of Cross & Cross. (The garage building still exists, but no longer houses cars.)

Because the full-floor and the partial-floor 11-room apartments enjoyed the sunny western exposure on Park Avenue, they were the first to rent. The less desirable eight-room units were nonetheless readily leased, as they were skillfully planned and graciously laid out. Like architect Rosario Candela, who was especially well known for vistas and strong diagonal axes in his apartment designs, Roth produced a handsome diagonal sightline from the entrance of the eight-room apartment that culminated at the living-room fireplace.

As time passed, large apartments became difficult to rent; the repercussions of the Great Depression hit even Park Avenue. Some of the 16-room apartments were subdivided, and four small penthouses were created, two of them duplexed from the top floor. But the building fared better than most.

When World War II restored the economy and the business environment boomed, Manhattan needed more office space. One by one the obsolete buildings fell before the wrecking ball, their sites immediately filled with much larger office buildings. In 1946, the first of these postwar structures went up on the site of the old Mayfair Apartments. Designed by the architectural firm of Kahn & Jacobs, 445 Park Avenue established the commercial beachhead that was to replace so many of the old apartment houses south of East 57th Street (*Figure 95*).

Some of the city's once-prestigious hotels—the Ambassador, the Marguery, the Park Lane—became memories. Two of the largest and grandest of Park Avenue's apartment houses, 270 and 277, were torn down when they could no longer produce a suitable financial return (*Figure 96*). The 46-foot living rooms at 290 Park Avenue and the 16-room apartments at 320 Park Avenue also had to go (*Figure 97*). So did other apartment houses Warren & Wetmore had designed for the New York Central Railroad, built as income-producing ventures on stilts over the train tracks below. Their beauty and grand accommodations simply could not provide the railroad with enough income, so they were replaced. Further up Park, the double building at 420–430, running the full block from East 55th to 56th Streets, was completely stripped down to its steel skeleton; a new office building was created in 1954 around the old frame-

Above, left: Figure 95. *445 Park Avenue, the 1946 office building, seen ca. 1960, that represented the beginning of the end for all the grand apartment houses to the south of it . . . all except Number 417. (Courtesy of Kahn & Jacobs.)* Above, right: Figure 96. *The entrance to the landscaped courtyard of 270 Park Avenue in 1918, since demolished for a block-square office tower. (Architecture magazine.)* Opposite: Figure 97. *Between the two World Wars lower Park Avenue looked like this photograph, ca. 1925: an unbroken row of block-long apartment houses with large suites, lavish fitments and real luxury accommodations. (Courtesy of the Museum of the City of New York.)*

work. (Ironically, Emery Roth's sons were the architects for the project.)

Through it all, the elegant old apartment house at 417 Park remained. Converted to cooperative ownership in 1946 and well maintained by the 28 owners, it was the only survivor, and is still the only residential building on Park between East 57th Street and Grand Central Terminal. It is likely to keep its unique char-

acter, too. More than a decade ago, the residents turned down yet another offer from a would-be developer. The price was the then-staggering sum of $32 million, representing the highest price offered for Manhattan land to that date—$3000 a square foot. Considering the subsequent rise in the value of those residents' apartments, their 1981 decision was a wise one.

Silent Sentinels

Limestone reticence along Fifth Avenue

IN 1910, THE *KANSAS CITY POST* ran a story, "A Western View of the New York Apartment House," which offered a distinctly Midwestern view of life in the big city at the turn of the century. Judging from the specifics, the subject of the ire of the Missouri newspaper's reporter was probably Alwyn Court:

For rent—suites of 14 rooms and five baths to suites of 34 rooms and nine baths. Rental, $6,500 to $12,000.

The buildings are 12 stories high and the apartments are arranged so that there are only one or two on the floor.

Each apartment is equipped with vacuum cleaners, dressing-rooms, millinery closets, plate-glass shelves, individual wine-vaults, cedar-lined closets, and every earthly and unearthly thing ever invented to make of a woman a useless parasite and of a man a restless, discontented Sybarite.

There's a man in livery to open the big front door. A man in livery to run the magnificent elevator. There are servants' quarters up under the roof, and there's an individual automobile garage in the basement for every individual flat.

What would you take to have to give up your home—your real home, with a yard for the baby to play in, and a porch for the dog to consider his bailiwick, and room enough on the hearthstone for the old gray cat, and a place up in the garret to hang your old fishing poles, and a corner in the basement to put the littlest boy's sled and the biggest girl's roller skates?

For rent—Suites of 14 rooms and five baths. Rentals, $6,500 to $12,000.

For rent—Do you know what signs ought to go alongside that one?

For rent—An empty heart.

For rent—A vacant brain.

For rent—An idle life.

Keep your $12,000-a-year flat, New York. Build all of them you want. Set them up in rows along Riverside Drive as a light-hearted child sets up his blocks along the ledge of his nursery window.

Fill up your apartment houses, your $12,000-a-year flats, with $12,000-a-year people.

Pack 'em in, crowd 'em in, push 'em in, 50 feet deep if you have to, a hundred feet deep if you must. They're nothing but coops, those big flats, anyway. Keep them in your own yard, poor, little old New York.

We don't want 'em out West, where the real people live—the real people who'd rather have a little four-room cottage with a yard and an old walnut tree at the corner of the house, and a rosy face at the window, than all the $12,000-a-year flats in the world.

Sic transit gloria vitæ rusticæ.

But what of those flats that caused such anger in Missouri? A ten-block stroll down Fifth Avenue from East 72nd Street will bring you face to face with some of the worst offenders: cooperative apartment houses of surpassing luxury that are in marked contrast to the ostentatious display of wealth so common in the earlier days of the robber barons' palaces they replaced. Erected during the first third of the twentieth century, they are quietly elegant in a very restrained manner, carefully hiding the nature of the apartments within. Who built them? Why? And who has lived within those guarded portals?

907 Fifth Avenue, located at East 72nd Street, won

the 1916 Gold Medal Award of the American Institute of Architects. The building's designer, J. E. R. Carpenter, originally created two apartments for each floor—a fact that would certainly have incensed our Missouri writer *(Figure 98)*. The top floor comprised a single 28-room unit with 11 rooms for servants. It rented for $30,000 a year at a time when a lesser family could live elsewhere in a more conventional three-bedroom unit for one-thirtieth that price. The rent control laws of 1943 put a crimp in the profits to be made even from apartments such as these, and between 1950 and 1960 the apartments of 907 Fifth Avenue were subdivided. The building now has as many as six units on each story.

Carpenter was one of the more active architects of the period. He designed 845 Fifth Avenue (also known as 4 East 66th Street) in 1920. So quietly detailed as to be almost bleak (if 11 stories of lime-

stone on Fifth Avenue could possibly be so), it houses but a single 18-room apartment to a floor *(Figure 99)*. The pair of reception spaces that comprise the living room of each apartment overlooks Central Park and encompasses a vast 1650 square feet. So elegant and refined are the units that, when the 94-year-old Bernard Baruch died in 1965, his fourth-floor suite commanded the then-astonishing price of $200,000.

A block and a half south is a discreet limestone pile designed by another specialist in rarified residential restraint, Rosario Candela *(Figure 100)*. Built by the prolific developer Anthony Campagna, 834 has a high preponderance of duplexes, with no more than three units to a floor, and was known for many years for housing senior members of the Rockefeller family. A little-known fact is that it was planned as a smaller midblock building, but after the steelwork was already in place, the developer unexpectedly was able to

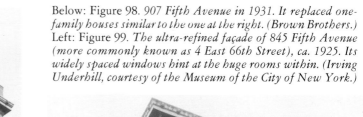
Below: Figure 98. *907 Fifth Avenue in 1931. It replaced one-family houses similar to the one at the right. (Brown Brothers.)* Left: Figure 99. *The ultra-refined façade of 845 Fifth Avenue (more commonly known as 4 East 66th Street), ca. 1925. Its widely spaced windows hint at the huge rooms within. (Irving Underhill, courtesy of the Museum of the City of New York.)*

purchase the grand mansion on the corner. That elegant, almost-new residence was summarily taken down and 834 Fifth Avenue was extended 25 feet to the corner of East 64th Street.

In the next block, two adjoining buildings of similar appearance serve entirely different functions. At 825 Fifth Avenue, also by J. E. R. Carpenter and completed in 1926, two- and three-room pieds-à-terre are provided for those whose living habits do not extend to cooking. Definitely not a "four-room cottage with a yard and an old walnut tree at the corner of the house," each apartment has a postage stamp of a serving pantry, with meal service obtainable from a central kitchen for consumption in the apartments or in the ground-floor dining room.

Next door, at 820 Fifth Avenue, architects Starrett and Van Vleck designed a 12-story version of an Italian

Renaissance palazzo, built by the Fred T. Ley Company in 1916 *(Figure 101)*. Although externally similar to 907 Fifth (completed the same year), and to 825 next door, Number 820 contains a single 18-room apartment on each floor. These rarified digs change hands only infrequently, and are decorated with a museum-like splendor barely hinted at by the polished bronze-grilled entrance doors and the meticulously maintained flowering front-yard trees and shrubs set in a lush bed of grass along Fifth Avenue.

Passing yet another one-flat-per-floor limestone block at 817 Fifth, a pedestrian will find 810 Fifth Avenue at the north corner of East 62nd Street *(Figure 102)*.

Bricken Construction Company, better known for erecting high-rise office buildings, erected this one, hiring the man who had already done so much on the avenue: J. E. R. Carpenter. Completed in 1926 as a replacement for a pair of brownstone-fronted private houses, Number 810 has an unusual entrance. Instead of a more conventional canopied awning, its side-street entryway employs a grand iron marquee. Carpenter's skill at creating elegant residential accommodations is seen in the building's elevations. The façade is a three-part composition echoing the Classical columns' base, shaft and capital. The four-story base section includes pediments, arches and balustrades, all set against a rusticated limestone-block wall. Paired windows emphasize the primary spaces on each floor.

The seven-story main section is rendered in planar limestone sheets, relieved only by stone quoins at the corners of the structure. The plainness of this portion of 810 is now accentuated by the modern replacement windows, which substitute plate-glass expanses for the multimullioned panes of the original windows. The upper section of the building is marked by double cornices and a balustrade along the roofline.

The careful detailing of the façade was carried into the entrance lobby, which was decorated with elaborate stonelike walls, bronze torchères and a carved plaster-work ceiling *(Figure 103)*. Upstairs, each single-apartment floor was minimally detailed, to permit the personal decorating tastes of the purchasers to take precedence. What the suites may have lacked in expensive materials, however, was more than made up for in space—almost 5000 square feet for each apartment. With four bedrooms, four servants' rooms, living and dining rooms and library, each flat was well equipped for luxurious living and entertaining. Original prices for the 13-room apartments ranged from

Figure 100. *The limestone elegance of 834 Fifth Avenue, ca. 1950. The arched double-height window high on the south façade lights the stairwell of a duplex. (Wurts Brothers, courtesy of the Museum of the City of New York.)*

Left: Figure 101. *820 Fifth Avenue in September 1926 as the town houses at the left were being razed to make way for the new apartment tower at 825 Fifth. (Wurts Brothers, courtesy of the Museum of the City of New York.)* Above: Figure 102. *810 Fifth Avenue, as presented in the building's original sales-promotion brochure. (Collection of Andrew Alpern.)*

$72,000 to $97,000, with monthly maintenance charges running about $800 for each suite.

The location was touted in the building's pro-spectus—and might have given the *Kansas City Post* more cause for attack if its writer had read it:

> The southern exposure is permanently assured while nothing can ever obstruct the lovely view of the Park. This picturesque bit of country right in the heart of New York is at your very door. From your windows overlooking the park, you will have during the spring a foreground of green and the bright surface of a lake. In the winter the scene changes to a constantly varying patchwork of green and white. This bit of country is a permanent feature of your home at 810 Fifth Avenue.

The sales brochure went on to discuss the con-venience of the IRT and the BMT (Brooklyn–Man-hattan Transit) subway stations nearby.

Perhaps the combination of both bucolic and urban amenities led Nelson Rockefeller to create a triplex penthouse in the building for his first wife, Mary Todhunter Clark, and himself. It was here that he raised his first family, and it was this apartment he most considered home, despite houses in Westchester County's Pocantico Hills and in Venezuela. He liked it so much, in fact, that he did not move out after his divorce.

As part of the settlement, he kept the lowest floor of the triplex, while his wife retained the upper two levels and converted them to a duplex for her own use.

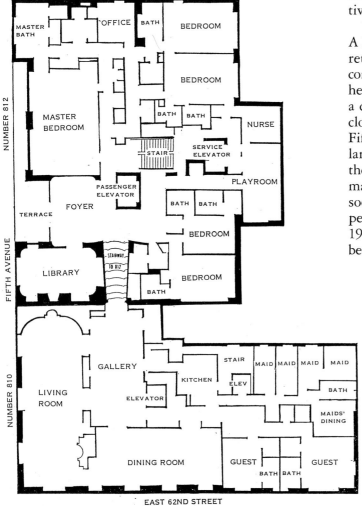

To provide for his second wife, Margaretta Fitler ("Happy") Murphy, and her children, Rockefeller expanded his one floor at 810 by connecting it to a full floor he purchased in the newly constructed building at 812 next door. Because of floor-level differences, a half-flight of steps was needed between the two sections of the sprawling 12,000-square-foot complex *(Figure 104)*. Sensitive to the first wife, Rockefeller and his second wife planned their new home so that they could use the 812 Fifth Avenue entrance, thereby avoiding the possibility of chance encounters in the elevator of Number 810.

In 1963, former Vice President Richard Nixon purchased the fifth-floor apartment at 810 Fifth Avenue, taking possession not long after Happy and Nelson Rockefeller had moved into their own new home. At the time, Nixon denied that his move from California to New York was for political reasons, asserting, "I'm going to New York for the purpose of practicing law and not for practicing politics."

Five years later, however, Nixon found himself battling Rockefeller for the Presidency of the United States. During the political fight, the two contenders used different elevators to gain access to their respective apartments.

The world turned, and Nixon moved out of the city. A lifetime later, seemingly, he came back. In 1979 he returned again to New York. Finding the hurdle of conservative cooperative boards quite insurmountable, he discovered that only money was needed to purchase a condominium, and he signed a contract to buy the closest thing he could find to what he had had at 810 Fifth Avenue. That was a comparably sized and similarly arranged 13-room apartment at Number 817 at the opposite end of the block, owned by one-time mayoral hopeful Abe Hirschfeld. But instead, Nixon soon took a house in Saddle River, New Jersey, perhaps pining for the sort of simple rusticity that the 1910 Missourians so loved—and which has always been alien to Fifth Avenue.

Left, top: Figure 103. *An artist's rendering of the lobby of 810 Fifth Avenue, presumably showing the sorts of people who were expected to buy apartments in the building.* (Collection of Andrew Alpern.) Left, bottom: Figure 104. *The apartment of one-time United States Vice President Nelson Rockefeller and his second wife, combining the lowest level of his former triplex at 810 Fifth Avenue with a full floor adjoining at Number 812.* (Courtesy of the New York Daily News.)

Built to Suit

Custom planning at 1107 Fifth Avenue

PERCEPTIONS OF THE "RIGHT" place to live probably date back to the days of the cave dwellers, when status-conscious families wanted to live on the sunny side of the mountain, close to the shelter of the most successful hunter. Things were not much different in New York during the years immediately following the end of World War I. The Upper East Side of Manhattan, on or near Fifth Avenue, was the only suitable place to live for socially aggressive New Yorkers, and the separate private residence was the pinnacle of achievement. As increasing numbers of people earned enough to approach this goal, however, property values and prices went so high that the one-family house in the best neighborhood became too expensive, even for the very rich.

The answer was the apartment house, with cooperative ownership offering the greatest degree of long-term stability and exclusivity. Catering to this market during this period, developers produced most of the city's finest apartment buildings, offering early buyers the opportunity to make changes to the basic plans of the units.

For those who chose to leverage their capital in ways other than buying, however, the choices were not as attractive—until 1925, that is, when opportunity arose on Fifth Avenue and East 92nd Street. Now a cooperative, 1107 Fifth was conceived and built as a rental building, but one with a difference. Renters were offered the chance to customize a standard apartment, or even to create as large an individual suite as they might desire *(Figure 105)*.

There had been a fundamental problem with overly customized cooperatives in the past: The integrity of the building's façade design was frequently compromised by the different tenants' demands, as illustrated by architect W. Fletcher White in a magazine cartoon titled "A Cooperative Apartment House Built to Meet the Owners' Tastes" *(Figure 106)*. At 1107 Fifth Avenue, the architects were determined that this would not happen. Yet they did want residents to be able to mold the interior space to their concepts of home life.

It was a problem these architects could handle: Well experienced with complex and lavish apartment houses (they had already designed many of the finest in the city), William Lawrence Rouse and Lafayette Anthony Goldstone had been partners since 1909. Over the years, they had parlayed their skills in working with architectural designs and with individual taste into a lucrative professional practice.

The idea for the building was born in the autumn of 1923, when General John Reed Kilpatrick of the George A. Fuller Construction Company and Douglas Gibbons of the eponymous real-estate firm met with Mrs. Edward F. Hutton. Mr. and Mrs. Hutton were then living in the former I. T. Burden house at the corner of East 92nd Street and Fifth Avenue. Mrs. Hutton, who felt that the traffic noise and gasoline fumes were becoming increasingly unpleasant, said that she wanted to have her home rebuilt at the top of an apartment house. While this may be true, it is also possible that, given her finely tuned business sense, Mrs. Hutton also wanted to capitalize on the significantly appreciated value of her property.

Adjoining land was acquired to augment her 50-by-100-foot lot, and a 13-story (plus penthouse) building

Above, left: Figure 105. *1107 Fifth Avenue, in 1925, when new. The triple-arched driveway entrance on 92nd Street was for the exclusive use of the Edward F. Hutton family and their guests. All others used the more modest entry on the avenue, whose canopy had not yet been installed when this photograph was made. (Wurts Brothers, courtesy of the Museum of the City of New York.)* Above, right: Figure 106. *An architect's conception of how a cooperative apartment house might look if it were built to meet the tastes of all of its joint owners. (W. Fletcher White, architect.)*

was planned. The top three levels and a portion of the ground floor were devoted to the Huttons' "relocated" mansion.

Essentially, the architects designed the building around the Huttons' ideas for their new home. The public entrance was placed on Fifth Avenue to permit a private driveway and lobby to be constructed on East 92nd Street for the exclusive use of the Huttons and their guests. Upstairs, a grand 54-room residence was created that holds the record as the largest apartment ever constructed. Mirroring the size and splendor of the rest of the apartment was the foyer, in the form of a Greek cross, with extreme dimensions of 44 feet by 44 feet *(Figure 107)*. The other entertaining rooms were scaled accordingly, with suitably high ceilings, elaborate moldings and wood paneling *(Figures 108 & 109)*. The apartment included a silver room, a wine room and cold-storage rooms for flowers and for furs, along with a self-contained suite of rooms for Mrs. Hutton's parents, Mr. and Mrs. Post (whose fortune

came from the breakfast cereal Post Toasties). There were outdoor sleeping porches connected to the separate bedrooms of Mr. Hutton and his wife, and the top floor included terrace play areas for the Hutton children. In all, there was more space in the new Hutton apartment than there had been in the old Hutton house on the site.

As soon as the plans for this apartment were complete, the developers sought tenants for the rest of the building. A "typical" floor plan was prepared, comprising two 13-room apartments. While these suites could hardly be considered cramped, only three floors were ever built in a form resembling the "typical" arrangement.

The space not devoted to the Hutton spread was apportioned to yield some impressive residences. The sixth floor, for example, was rented to John W. Davis, Democratic Presidential candidate in 1924, and to Mrs. Isaac Newton Seligman, widow of the son of the founder of the Seligman banking house and herself a

Loeb of the Kuhn Loeb banking firm. Mrs. Seligman used space from what might have been part of Davis' apartment (had it been "typical") to create a 30-by-36-foot living room, and transformed the rest of the place into a one-bedroom unit of more than 5000 square feet (with six rooms for servants).

The prominent surgeon Dr. John Adolf Vietor took a complete apartment on the eighth floor and half an apartment on the ninth for a duplex that included a 19-by-38-foot library and a comparably sized drawing room.

Charles van Vleck had a similar arrangement on floors three and four, but went one better by making his drawing room two stories high with a viewing balcony at the second level.

The apartment that comprised the entire north half of the tenth and eleventh floors included a double-height drawing room 24 by 36 feet, and was arranged to provide a vista of more than 100 feet that encompassed drawing room, gallery, library, dining room and aviary. Sharing floors ten and 11 was the corresponding duplex of roller-bearing industrialist William R. Timkin and his wife, which was only slightly less impressive.

Even the more "normal" apartments in the building were given special custom touches. Spacious sewing rooms were provided in the suites taken by Lindley Garrison, Secretary of War under President Woodrow Wilson, and by J. Montgomery Hare, a lawyer also active in politics. The fourth-floor apartment of Mrs. Joseph Dilworth, whose husband had made his fortune in wholesale groceries, was rearranged to allow for a valet's room and a windowed "pressing room." And the space devoted to closets in each apartment was, by today's standards, sufficient to create a good-sized one-bedroom unit.

Size and accoutrements aside, these residences were particularly unusual because they were built to suit on a rental basis under leases that ran for only five to eleven years. The Hutton apartment was the exception, with a 15-year term. Original rentals (with no escalation provisions) were $8000 to $30,000 per year; the Hutton spread was $75,000 annually.

At the end of the Huttons' lease, the 54-room triplex was vacated, and it remained without a tenant for ten years. Ultimately, it was subdivided into six apartments, each rather more conventional than the Hutton place, but all quite spacious nonetheless. The space of the private Hutton lobby and concierge apartment was ultimately converted to medical offices. Some of the other units were altered and reapportioned over the years, but the building remains one of the more distinctive on the Upper East Side.

Figure 107. *The foyer of the triplex apartment of Mr. and Mrs. E. F. Hutton at 1107 Fifth Avenue, 1927. (J. C. Maugans, courtesy of Harmon H. Goldstone.)*

Above: Figure 108. *The drawing room of the Hutton apartment, 1927, with the stiff French formality typical of its time. (J. C. Maugans, courtesy of Harmon H. Goldstone.)* Below: Figure 109. *The Huttons' ponderously furnished dining room, 1927. A light meal would be unthinkable in such a space. (J. C. Maugans, courtesy of Harmon H. Goldstone.)*

Multiple Mansions

Stacked status behind the modest façade of
820 Park Avenue

AT 820 PARK AVENUE, ON the northwest corner of East 75th Street, sits a symbol of an era: multiple apartment-house "mansions" created by one of the more flamboyant publishers of his time.

The story begins in the 1920s, the last period of great house building in Manhattan. The reasons for the cessation were many. Following World War I, it became more difficult to obtain the staff needed to run a private house. Construction costs began to spiral upward. Building private homes was soon an unrealistic proposition for all but the richest of families.

In addition, as more and more people wanted to cluster within the confines of what were perceived as the "best" neighborhoods, land values soared higher and higher. The resulting tax hikes weighed heavily on the residents of single-family houses along Fifth and Park Avenues and on the side streets of the Upper East Side. Homeowners were assessed on what *could* be built on their property, rather than on what was actually there. They soon discovered that it was more economical to sell their land.

They found ready buyers in the new breed of apartment-house developers, who were prepared to pay large sums for the sites. Even those homeowners with very deep pockets were hard-pressed to resist the attractive offers, particularly when measured against the imperatives of the tax man.

Architect Harry Allan Jacobs summed up the feelings of many in the *New York Times* on November 1, 1925:

> It will be only a short time before the private house will be forgotten and a thing of the past. The rich man has found himself being hemmed in on all sides by high buildings, his light and air cut off, paying an excessive rent in the large fixed charge of the initial investment, taxes, repairs, and numerous servants necessary to maintain his private house environment.

The newer buildings could elevate the inhabitants high above the detrimental propinquity of automotive noise and pollution, and some of the worst of the security problems inherent in lavish street-level living styles. Add to that the chance to design a special residence high in the sky, with fresh air, cool breezes, abundant sunlight and expansive views, and the previous generation's requirement for a totally private roof over one's head became less and less important as the decade of the 1920s proceeded along its course. How could the mansions of old compete?

One tried—not ignoring, however, the styles of the age. In 1920, Mrs. Millbank Anderson hired architect John Mead Howells to design a new house at 820 Park Avenue. Howells produced an ultrarefined limestone box, 102 feet wide and 34 feet deep, with minimalist articulation and almost no exterior embellishment. The traditional Classical forms and detailing were so restrained that they were more a memory than a reality *(Figure 110)*. The building was bloodless, lacking any of the charm or exuberance of good Classical design.

Perhaps because of that, Mrs. Anderson never moved in. The building remained vacant until 1924, when Howells was retained to remodel and redecorate its interiors for a new owner, A. J. Kobler, the

Opposite, top: Figure 110. *A 1920 view of the short-lived limestone town house at 820 Park Avenue put up by Mrs. Millbank Anderson in 1920 and taken down five years later by A. J. Kobler. (Wurts Brothers, courtesy of the Museum of the City of New York.)* Opposite, bottom: Figure 111. *The living room of Mrs. Anderson's house, 1924, as decorated for A. J. Kobler. (Courtesy of the Museum of the City of New York.)* Right: Figure 112. *A 1946 view of the tower of stacked, multifloor apartments that replaced the Anderson-Kobler town house. (Wurts Brothers, courtesy of the Museum of the City of New York.)*

publisher of the Hearst organization's successful and influential *American Weekly (Figure 111).*

Kobler was too successful personally to be overly concerned with rising property taxes, and presumably got from his architect the sort of interior fitments he had wanted. Nonetheless, only a year later he tore the house down. The five-year rise and demise of the one-family 820 Park Avenue contrasts strongly with the 40-year life of the two modest row houses Mrs. Anderson had taken down to make room for her new building project. Clearly, that project represented the last gasp of the old ways of living in Manhattan.

Kobler sacrificed his own new home to make way for a thoroughly modern concept in apartment-house living: multiple mansions stacked one upon another for soaring status and expansive living. Expanding the depth of the house property to 51 feet with the purchase of an adjoining 1880s brownstone, Kobler had a buildable site.

His architect on the new project was Harry Allan Jacobs, who had handled commercial and hotel projects and was responsible for the Friars Club on East 55 Street. (His son Robert was equally successful as an architect in partnership was Ely Jacques Kahn.) Jacobs' particular forte was designing lavish Manhattan town houses. Having executed residential projects for Adolph Lewisohn, Otto Kahn, Herbert Lehman, Adolph Zucker and Martin Beck, he was well suited to devising a multiple dwelling of eight superimposed mansions.

Jacobs' apartment house was a simple rectangle, 14 stories high. Perhaps in reaction to the limestone chill of the previous residence on the site, this design is aggressively warm. The high base is veneered in a variegated, tan-colored sandstone, with the bulk of the structure laid in a darker Holland brick. Near the top are four massive balconies and other ornamental elements, all of stone in a color that blends with the brickwork *(Figure 112).*

The uppermost three-story section of the northern

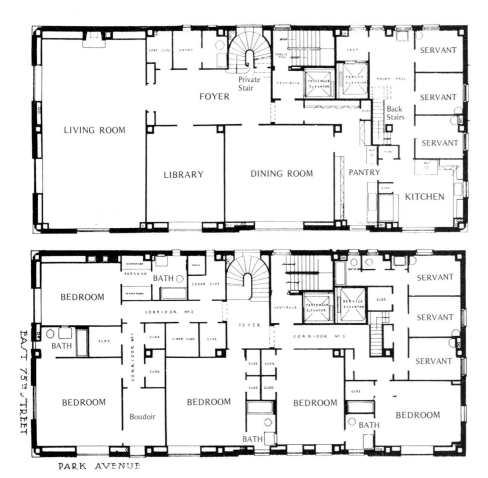

Figure 113. *A "typical" 17-room duplex apartment as originally designed for 820 Park Avenue. (Collection of Andrew Alpern.)*

half of the Park Avenue façade had a slate veneer above a partial cornice. The slate (which the architect asserted represented a "mansard," and has since been removed) created a towerlike effect at the building's southern end. (This presaged the setbacks and ornamentation introduced with the multiple-dwelling law of 1929.)

Although the tenants in Kobler's building took the opportunity to individualize their apartments (the architect prepared a different plan for each floor), there was a "typical" 17-room duplex unit. Comprising five master bedrooms, six servants' rooms, plus entertaining and storage spaces, each of these grand residences featured a 19-by-23-foot dining room, a 19-by-16-foot library and a 38-by-22-foot living room *(Figure 113)*.

By far the most outstanding plan at 820 Park Avenue was the triplex apartment that Kobler reserved for himself at the top of the building. Encompassing three full floors of 4000 square feet each, this "mansion-in-the-sky" included a huge drawing room with a 20-foot-high ceiling.

Contemporary descriptions of the Kobler home revealed decorations, furnishings and an architectural ambience worthy of a Gothic palace. The entrance hall had a low groin-vaulted ceiling set off with shallow

stone arches and richly carved doors. A stone Gothic stairway led up from the entrance hall to the library, and down to the dining room, which had stone walls, a massive stone fireplace and a coffered ceiling reproduced from the Uffizi Palace. But even the massive three-story stair, embellished with wrought iron from the forge of Samuel Yellin, paled beside the spectacular drawing room *(Figure 114)*.

Two stories high, the room was lighted by leaded and stained-glass windows and a large multiarmed chandelier. It served as a setting for Kobler's extensive collection of rare old French Gothic furniture and artworks, and was dominated by an exceptional 16th-century carved stone fireplace, which drew the eye up to a deeply carved and polychromed ceiling *(Figure 115)*. A profusion of stone arches offered views of a music alcove, the entrance hall and the great Gothic stairway.

The library on the floor above included a small stone oriel window looking down upon the drawing room and its wall-hung tapestry, whose previous owners are said to have included Henry VIII and Cardinal Wolsey *(Figure 116)*. The furniture had simiarly lofty pedigrees, boasting prior tenancy in the Strozzi and Barberini palaces.

Other rooms in the Kobler suite were equally grand,

Figure 114. *A corner of the drawing room in A. J. Kobler's triplex home in the apartment tower at 820 Park Avenue, 1928. (*Arts & Decoration *magazine, courtesy of The New-York Historical Society.)*

Above, left: Figure 115. *The huge two-storied Kobler drawing room with its massive stone fireplace and French Gothic furniture, 1928.* (Arts & Decoration *magazine, courtesy of The New-York Historical Society.*) Above, right: Figure 116. *A 1928 view of the Kobler drawing room showing the stone oriel window-balcony of the library.* (Arts & Decoration *magazine, courtesy of The New-York Historical Society.*)

with an eighteenth-century Venetian bedroom, bathrooms finished in African onyx and gold, and almost enough fifteenth- and sixteenth-century tapestries to fill a mini-Cloisters.

Mary Fanton Roberts, writing in the March 1928 issue of *Arts & Decoration,* gave this assessment, neatly summing up the hubris, optimism and extravagance of the period immediately preceding the crash of 1929:

There is the general impression today, and it seems quite justified by apartments like this one of Mr. and Mrs. Kobler, that there are no finer, more comfortable, more beautiful ways of living in the world than the New York apartment at its best. Now that houses are actually being built for duplex and triplex apartments, so that all the space and isolation to be found in the large country home can be achieved, with much less care and responsibility, there seems to be no end to the popularity of this very modern way of living luxuriously in a large city. And when it is possible for the very structure of an apartment to be designed and executed as a gracious and appropriate background

for the treasures that have been accumulated in the lifetime of very artistic people, it would seem as though the finer ideal of civilized life has been achieved.

A bit gushy to our ears, perhaps, but indicative of the increasingly optimistic outlook of the world that built up just prior to the Great Depression that was to begin less than two years later. A. J. Kobler at 820 Park Avenue, William Randolph Hearst at 137 Riverside Drive *(Figure 117)* and Arthur Brisbane at 1215 Fifth Avenue all built huge, lavishly decorated apartments, each with an astonishing two-storied drawing room. All three men were spectacularly successful publishers whose ego-fulfillment activities were almost full-time occupations. And all three men are gone, along with their grandly hubristic residences. We mourn the passing of those awesome apartments, forgetting, perhaps, that without the monomaniacal personalities of their creators, those apartments could never have been built.

Figure 117. *One of the* subsidiary *entertaining rooms in the apartment of William Randolph Hearst at 137 Riverside Drive, ca. 1929.* (*Hewitt-Smith, courtesy of The New-York Historical Society.*)

Magnificent Maisonette

Proudly palatial privacy at 666 Park Avenue

As the 1920s progressed, districts that had formerly been exclusively residential became more and more commercial, a destiny to which many areas of the city had been subject over the previous three centuries of Manhattan's development. Owners of most one-family row houses whose neighborhoods were no longer suitable for home ownership were content to buy apartments within the broad market of offerings being created by developers. Large apartments, duplexes, even triplexes or penthouses, were sufficient to lure the former house owners.

For those who dwelled in the huge mansions of Fifth Avenue the shift to multifamily living arrangements was not so readily made. They were used to distinctive residences and would not be satisfied with ordinary apartments, regardless how luxurious. With commercial development edging out existing residences all along Fifth Avenue south of East 59th Street, this market was significant, if not overly large.

One way of making apartment-house living comparable to the experience of living in a free-standing private mansion is to provide the equivalent of an individual house and then surround it with an apartment building. The resultant minihouse or maisonette can have the accommodations and convenience of the most lavish multifloored apartment along with the privacy inherent to a one-family home.

A very special maisonette was designed into the elegant limestone apartment house erected in 1927 at 660 Park Avenue by Starrett Brothers, Inc. In 1924, the company had retained architects Lafayette A. Goldstone and William L. Rouse to design the apartment house at 760 Park Avenue. Their plan must have

Right: Figure 118. *The restrained and formal limestone apartment house at 660 Park Avenue. The entire lower portion of the building defined by the narrow horizontal rustication banding comprises a single maisonette apartment. (Courtesy of the Museum of the City of New York.)* Opposite: Figure 119. *The private street entrance and separate address of the maisonette apartment within 660 Park Avenue. Entry to the other apartments in the building is through the door to the right. (Hewitt-Smith, courtesy of The New-York Historical Society.)*

particularly pleased Starrett, because the company evidently instructed the architectural firm of York and Sawyer to use the same arrangement for 660 Park Avenue, planned only two years later.

York and Sawyer was a firm better known for its grandly elegant banks, including the august Central Savings Bank (now of changed name) at West 73rd Street and Broadway, and the incomparable Romanesque Revival Bowery Savings Bank (also recently renamed) on East 42nd Street at Pershing Square. It was also responsible for the original section of The New-York Historical Society at Central Park West and West 77th Street.

For 660 Park Avenue, the firm designed a very restrained and formal interpretation in limestone of the architecture of the Italian Renaissance. Appearing as a slim tower, 660 Park's design featured balustraded stone belt courses and changes in surface texture to delineate and separate the ground floor, the portion of

the building devoted to the maisonette, the main section of the structure and the special top-floor apartment that was duplexed to the roof. If you could read these signs, which also included two-story-high windows and two double-doored entrances, you could see on the outside what was going on within. But overall, the building gave the appearance of being just another of the grand and refined apartment houses that were rapidly replacing the brownstones of an earlier Park Avenue *(Figure 118)*.

The maisonette was the architect's special assignment. But it has had an odd history. Apparently, it has had only four owners, the first of whom may never have lived in it.

On June 27, 1926, Virginia Pope reported in the *New York Times* Sunday magazine that Mrs. William Kissam Vanderbilt II would be moving into a maisonette at 660 Park Avenue. While no mention was made of the separate address of the maisonette *(Figure 119)*,

its identifying number of 666 Park Avenue would have been appropriate for Mrs. Vanderbilt, who was then living in her McKim, Mead & White town house at 666 Fifth Avenue.

According to Virginia Pope, the triplex was to have a 22-by-46-foot living room and a dining room "almost as large." There was to be an 18-by-23-foot library, and these entertaining rooms were to have 18-foot ceilings. Seven bedrooms were to be provided, along with "conveniently placed" dressing rooms. An article in the *New York Times* the following year stated that the $185,000 Mrs. Vanderbilt had paid for the maisonette was the highest price ever paid for an apartment at the time of its purchase.

There is no evidence, however, that Mrs. Vanderbilt ever actually moved in. The first person whose occupancy of the apartment has been verified is Seton Porter, a wealthy corporation executive. In 1928 Porter hired the architects William R. Pearsall, J. Layng Mills and F. Burrall Hoffman, Jr., to make alterations and presumably decorate the dwelling. In 1981, a speculation was made in an article in the *Times* that Porter may have been attracted to the maisonette's high-ceilinged living room because he had previously lived at 14 East 75th Street, which the reporter called a "fine apartment building with grand, double-height living rooms." It is indeed such a building, but it was not likely to have provided spatial inspiration to Porter since it was not erected until 1929, *after* he had moved to Park Avenue.

The "apartment" that Porter did move into has a double-doored entrance on the street level adjoining the portal to the common apartment house lobby. A flight of broad marble steps leads to a foyer at the *piano nobile*. From here a grand oval staircase sweeps past a mezzanine, where the plans called for two guest rooms, five servants' rooms and extensive storage. The stair continues up to the fourth floor, where the original plans indicated there were three bedrooms with their ancillary dressing rooms and baths, along with five more servants' rooms and further storage. Also indicated were two sets of back stairs, one accessing an intermediate demimezzanine over the butler's pantry for storing china and glassware, and the other ending in a spacious servants' hall and general receiving area adjoining the goods elevator, the kitchen and the pantry.

The heart and splendor of 666 Park Avenue are the three primary entertaining rooms: the library, dining

Left, top: Figure 120. *The Louis XIII room in 1929. (Hewitt-Smith, courtesy of The New-York Historical Society.)* Left, bottom: Figure 121. *The same space a half-century later. (Courtesy of Sotheby Parke Bernet.)*

room and living room. All have extra-high ceilings, fireplace mantels and special detailing. The decoration of these spaces may have been the work of Seton Porter's consultants, or they may have been originally installed for Mrs. Vanderbilt and "inherited" when Porter bought the apartment. Either way, they were appropriately lavish, to suit the rooms' grand proportions, and the seigniorial touch extended throughout the residence *(Figures 120 & 121).* The library was paneled in the Georgian mode, with the room featuring a well-carved fireplace and overmantel taken from an eighteenth-century London house *(Figures 122 & 123).* The dining room was embellished with a ceramic fireplace surround and lit by a huge Russian chandelier and matching wall sconces.

The grandest part by far, however, was the living room *(Figure 124).* Magnificently paneled with seventeenth-century pine woodwork brought over from a large English house, the room featured an elaborately carved mantelpiece with a complementary overmantel and flanking Corinthian pilasters *(Figure 125).* As Seton Porter furnished the maisonette, it could support huge parties as well as intimate evenings, and it was clearly a *home* rather than merely a musuem.

Leslie and Fan Samuels both had significant resources gained from mercantile activities, and in later years contributed heavily to the Lincoln Center for the Performing Arts, funding a major renovation of the Vivian Beaumont and New York State Theaters. In 1938, Mr. and Mrs. Samuels bought the Porter apartment. Retaining virtually all the installations of the previous tenant, they merely added their own furnishings and artwork, acquired over years of discerning travel. Their taste was domestically scaled, and gave them a warmly congenial home environment. The maisonette served the couple well for more than 40 years of collecting and entertaining. When his wife died, however, Samuels found the rooms too filled with memories, and left for a relatively small suite in the Waldorf Towers. He then arranged for Sotheby's to catalogue and auction off all the art and furnishings.

Only days before the house was to be stripped, Samuels was told that a woman wanted to view the contents. Mishearing the name, Samuels thought she was the wife of Texas retailer Stanley Marcus. Instead, Imelda Marcos showed up with a retinue of bodyguards and hangers-on. She strode through the house with little apparent interest, but then offered to buy everything in the place for a flat figure. Following a

Right, top: Figure 122. *The library as furnished for Seton Porter, 1929. (Hewitt-Smith, courtesy of The New-York Historical Society.)* Right, bottom: Figure 123. *The library in 1981 when it was home to Leslie Samuels. (Courtesy of Sotheby Parke Bernet.)*

Opposite: Figure 124. *The south end of the living room as furnished in 1929 for Seton Porter. (Hewitt-Smith, courtesy of The New-York Historical Society.)* Above: Figure 125. *The fireplace area of the drawing room as furnished by Mr. and Mrs. Samuels. (Courtesy of Sotheby Parke Bernet.)*

series of negotiating sessions, the deal was made. Marcos asserted that she wanted the art and furniture for a museum so that her people could enjoy the accoutrements of the rich. The museum never materialized, Imelda and Ferdinand Marcos fled their country, and the Samuels' former possessions were scattered.

Disposing of his longtime home was even more difficult. Taking into account the maintenance charges on the cooperative apartment that then amounted to $77,000 a year, he set its price at $9 million and called in the Sotheby's real-estate arm to market it. The listing sat for months. Apparently, it was too costly for all but foreign diplomats, Middle Eastern potentates and rock stars of wide notoriety. Since such people would not pass muster in front of the cooperative's board of directors, no sale was in the offing.

Sotheby's suggested that Samuels lower his price, and named a figure significantly below the original.

Samuels blanched, and said he would telephone the following day with an answer. He then rang up his old and close friend, the polymath and philanthropist Dr. Arthur Sackler, and asked him what he thought of the reduction. Sackler replied without hesitation that he would be right over with his checkbook. His offer was not in jest; he did in fact purchase the maisonette. He then spent more than two years renovating and redecorating before finally moving in. He lived there for a relatively brief time, however, before he died.

But the magnificent maisonette still lives, and one might hope that New York will always need such a residence. Notwithstanding its original ten servants' rooms, the dwelling does not require a large staff and is thus a realistic home for anyone with wealth and the right credentials who wants expansive space. May it continue for many generations to provide such a home to as many successive tenants as fate may dictate!

Penthouse Podium

Rus in urbe *atop 1010 Fifth Avenue*

PENTHOUSE LIVING WAS RELATIVELY new in 1922, most apartment-house roofs being given over to elevator machinery and water tanks. Occasionally they were also used to accommodate janitors' apartments or additional servants' rooms, but rooftop living for socially self-conscious New Yorkers was almost unheard-of.

This changed dramatically when publisher Condé Nast brought together high-life parties and high-level living. In 1923, architects Delano & Aldrich filed plans for a new apartment house at 1040 Park Avenue for the J. H. Taylor Construction Company *(Figure 126)*. There were to be three units on each floor, with additional maids' rooms on the roof. In 1924, before those upper spaces could be constructed, the plans were changed to provide a grand duplex for Nast. The corner unit on the top floor was redesigned as private family quarters and connected by a simple staircase to the rooftop entertaining salons, all of which were decorated in the French manner by Elsie de Wolfe. Completed in 1925, the penthouse was inaugurated with the first of Condé Nast's many lavish parties, made famous as much by the guest lists as by the entertainment.

The self-made maverick real-estate developer Frederick Fillmore French was also a pioneer in rooftop living. He created a triplex penthouse for his family at 1140 Fifth Avenue, a building he constructed in 1922, but he did not live there long. Perhaps taking his inspiration from Condé Nast, or merely desiring more outdoor play space for his four children at a venue closer to his office, French carried the penthouse concept several steps further.

At 1010 Fifth Avenue, on the north corner of East 82nd Street, he designed a 15-story apartment house with four units on each floor, ranging from seven to 12 rooms *(Figure 127)*. As the buildings of Fifth Avenue go, there is nothing particularly impressive or unusual

Opposite: Figure 126. *1040 Park Avenue, in which Condé Nast's duplex penthouse made rooftop living chic in 1925. (Wurts Brothers, courtesy of the Museum of the City of New York.)* Above: Figure 127. *A 1939 view of the apartment house at 1010 Fifth Avenue that Fred F. French constructed as the podium for a 14-room penthouse to house his family. (Wurts Brothers, courtesy of the Museum of the City of New York.)*

Above: Figure 128. *One corner of the French penthouse atop 1010 Fifth Avenue as it appeared in the late 1930s when occupied by E. Cochrane Bowen. The steel-and-glass wind-screen was taken down during World War II, but it was recreated at half its old height by the present owner of the penthouse. (Richard Averill Smith, courtesy of The New-York Historical Society.)* Left: Figure 129. *A view ca. 1938 of the rooftop fountain in which the French children were reported to have sailed toy boats. (Richard Averill Smith, courtesy of The New-York Historical Society.)*

about 1010—nothing, that is, except the penthouse. Indeed, the entire structure might almost be considered a grand podium on which the new French family estate was to sit *(Figure 128)*.

French's wife Cordelia described her "country life within the city" in an article she wrote for *The Voice,* the house organ of her husband's firm:

From both door and windows [of the penthouse apartment] one may gaze upon a suburban scene, grass lawns, flowers, shrubs, trees, and a sprinkling of butterflies. . . At one end, the lion of the fountain [*Figure 129*] looks benignly down upon a toy flotilla in the pool beneath. Here, far above the policeman's whistle, three little boys find a variety of outdoor games, Tired of shipping, they engage in fortress building in the sandbox, with now and then a race up the awning strings with caterpillars. . . . As the season changes and the snow flies, all hands are out with shovels and the hot water hose to make a clearing. Traffic relieved, attention is soon diverted to a snowman. But most welcome of all are the first days

Above: Figure 130. *The living room of the penthouse apartment when occupied by the French family, ca. 1928. (Courtesy
of the Museum of the City of New York.)* Right: Figure 131. *A
hallway of the French apartment at 1010 Fifth Avenue, ca.
1928. (Courtesy of the Museum of the City of New York.)*

of spring. Every size and weight of garden tool is then
employed as "Dad" and his gang of youthful workmen
mix soil with sand and fertilizer. What a joyful mixing
performance it is! The earth is then distributed and
each, standing in front of his own particular forcing
box, sows his favorite seeds. A few weeks later the
green young shoots are carefully removed from the
boxes and planted in their permanent beds in the
garden, just as it is done by the "best families" down
on the earth. A complete roof, it seems, should never
be without a handball court. Here the tired business
man, in his walled arena, is "fattened for the slaughter"
of the next business day. Here, before dinner, he
gyrates with his trainer, getting up the all-essential
"good old sweat." Mark you, however, he is a martyr,
not a handball player, for play must ever be cloaked in
the dignity of preparation for work.

Therein, of course, lies the secret of French's career:
constant hard work aimed always at furthering his
business. There was always time (and money) enough,
however, to make his daughter and three sons com-

Figure 132. *A portion of the terrace surrounding the French penthouse as it appeared about 1964. (Adrien Boutrelle and William Sevecke.)*

fortable—comfort that French, a poor boy from the Bronx, had not known as a child *(Figures 130 & 131)*.

The *rus in urbe* atop 1010 Fifth Avenue was his urban ruse; country living within striking distance of his office. Such accommodations were not done easily. According to contemporary accounts an extra 40 tons of structural steel supported the 135 tons of soil and natural greenery of the "country" environment. Copper flashings protected the building from the dampness of the garden earth, and a system of copper leaders and cast-iron pipes conducted excess rain and melted snow down to the sewer mains. Finally, a massive steel-and-glass windscreen rendered the rooftop usable in all but the most blustery weather.

The 14-room penthouse suite was home to Fred and Cordelia French, to John Winslow French, Fred, Jr., and Theodore, and to Ellen Millard French, who became Mrs. Ernest McKay. (The Millard in the daughter's name and the Fillmore in the father's commemorated a distant relationship to that less-than-memorable president.)

Developer Fred F. French died suddenly of a heart attack in 1936 at the age of 52. His bucolic rooftop living could not protect him from his own hard-driving pace of work. His carefully constructed suburban estate high over Fifth Avenue was preserved, and was restored in 1988 by its longtime owner. In addition to rebuilding the apartment's interior, she recreated to a six-foot height French's 12-foot windscreen, which had been taken down in the 1940s.

By 1981, however, the French family's tenancy and the well-constructed underpinnings of their garden had been long forgotten *(Figure 132)*. That year, problems in two apartments on the floor below prompted the cooperative's board of directors to remove the entire planted area. Repairs were made,

and the garden recreated to the extent possible with new plantings.

Complaints from below nonetheless continued, and a lawsuit ensued. The board's engineer declared that the roof was in danger of imminent collapse. Faced with conflicting testimony from the penthouse owner's own engineers, the judge ordered the entire rooftop garden removed and stored, and the naked roof structure tested.

This was done, but the engineers again had opposing opinions. The board claimed that the garden was not original and was a danger to the building's structural integrity. It asserted that the rooftop tenant had no right to a restored garden and ought to pay for all the repair work.

At this point the penthouse occupant hired historian Christopher Gray as an architectural detective to ferret out the real story of these modern-day Hanging Gardens of Babylon. Gray's digging led him to the family scrapbooks of the two surviving French children, in which home snapshots proved that the garden had been there from the beginning. He unearthed original construction documents and contemporary newspaper articles showing that proper structural and waterproofing provisions had been made. With the Gray report in hand, the court then ordered the board to make the required roof repairs at its own expense and to restore the planted areas.

The penthouse at 1010 Fifth Avenue now provides a living (if private) monument to Fred F. French, a man who has been honored for his construction of Tudor City, Knickerbocker Village and his own exuberant neo-Assyrian office building at 551 Fifth Avenue. His impact on the concept of urban penthouse living may ultimately prove to have been his most enduring memorial.

Bulky Beresford

Classically triple-towered and terraced at
211 Central Park West

THE 1920S WAS A heady era: flivvers and flappers were the froth, while the effervescent brew beneath rose higher and higher. The Great War with the Kaiser was over and so, it seemed, was war for all time. Anything other than peace and prosperity was unthinkable. Business was booming, the financial markets yielded profits almost effortlessly, and construction was feverish.

Taller and more lavish apartment houses were being built, but not everyone could live in them—or build them. Many of the grandest (primarily on the East Side) were organized as cooperatives to exclude "undesirables." If you were Jewish, accomplishments and money were often ignored by real-estate brokers, with ugly stereotyping blocking your way to the sort of apartment you might consider suitable.

Such barriers extended to business. The prestigious American Institute of Architects had been founded in 1857 almost as much as a social club as a professional organization. It catered to the needs of an elite and well-educated membership, and over the years had permitted very few Jews to join its ranks and append the coveted "AIA" to their names. Emery Roth was chagrined to discover this when he was rejected for membership in 1927.

Roth was an immigrant from the Austro-Hungarian Empire who had arrived alone, in the United States in 1884, age 13. Although he began with less than eight dollars to his name, he worked imaginatively and very hard, and built himself up in a scenario that even Horatio Alger would have considered incredible. With boundless enthusiasm and endless energy and talent, Roth worked his way through several prestigious architectural design offices and into his own practice, Stein, Cohen & Roth, in 1898. His first major building was the Hotel Belleclaire, completed in 1903 at Broadway and West 77th Street. Still standing, it has official recognition from the New York City Landmarks Preservation Commission.

It was obvious even in 1903 that Roth could create landmark-quality buildings, and he received a succession of increasingly important commissions, many from the prominent developers Bing & Bing. When Roth felt he had accomplished enough to be ready for membership in the prestigious establishment of the AIA, he ran headlong into its prejudices against Jews, immigrants and self-taught architects. Rallying the support of fellow architect Thomas Hastings, whose social and professional credentials were impeccable, he finally gained admission after several months of politicking. Roth's own social difficulties must have influenced his attitudes as an architect. Perhaps it gave him added incentive when he was asked to design a replacement for the nineteenth-century Hotel Beresford at the corner of West 81st Street and Central Park West.

In 1884, José de Navarro sought to expand his development empire beyond his eight-building project on Central Park South. He filed plans for four 12-story apartment buildings on Central Park West from West 81st to 82nd Streets. He was overextended, however, and ultimately abandoned the venture. Alva Walker

Figure 133. *The original Hotel Beresford of 1889. (Collection of Andrew Alpern.)*

later acquired the property, and erected a six-story Hotel Beresford in 1889 *(Figure 133),* later expanding it with a ten-story addition to encompass the entire blockfront between West 81st and 82nd Streets. It was one of several large "family" apartment-hotels along Central Park West. Hotels, institutions and early grand-luxe apartment houses such as the Dakota, the Prasada and the Langham were what the high speculator-driven land values demanded. One-family row houses on Central Park West were not economically prudent, and very few were built.

Kept away from the East Side by social pressures, affluent Jewish New Yorkers looked more and more to the Upper West Side for luxurious apartments. Roth himself lived there. He had already proven his ability to produce the sort of architectural accommodation this market demanded, and so was hired by HRH Construction Company to design the new Beresford.

Improvements to Central Park West doubtless influenced the decision to build. The trolley tracks had been removed, the avenue widened, and the Independent (IND) subway was being built, with a station at West 81st Street. Since the old Beresford no longer met the needs of the times, its site was expanded with the acquisition of four large row houses adjoining on

West 81st Street and four smaller ones on West 82nd. This gave Roth an enviable site. Facing Central Park on one side, and Manhattan Square and the American Museum of Natural History on the other, the building would get uninterrupted daily sunlight. Roth had an opportunity to create a monument that could be seen and recognized from afar.

And what a creation! Roth scholar Steven Ruttenbaum described the Beresford as "a massive pile of Classical elements, skillfully composed." At 200 feet square and 22 stories high, it is massive indeed. Over the steel structural framework is a huge pile of material: granite, marble, limestone, terra-cotta and brick. The Classical elements are profuse, lavish and bold. They enliven the façade, articulate its parts and contribute a dignified vigor to the overall impression.

The Beresford's decorative treatment is late Italian Renaissance. Applied over a heroic and complex underlying form, this yields a solid, striking and self-assured building, a cube surmounted by corner towers, which in turn surround more building mass. That spatial concept might alone offer the impression of a fortress *(Figure 134).* The grandeur comes in the embellishment.

As do many Classically inspired apartment houses

in the city, the Beresford sits on a three-story rusticated limestone base. Here the base is pierced by four entrances with grandly conceived and boldly executed framing. Broken pediments, strongly modeled cartouches and delicate bas-relief are carved in the limestone and are complemented by bronze lanterns and doors.

Rising from there is the beige brick bulk with prudently plain casement windows (any repetitive embellishment would have been overwhelming and would have detracted from the strength of the composition). A multitude of skillfully placed decorative elements articulate, emphasize and enhance the basic building form. There are belt courses, stone balustrades, iron railings, rosettes and cartouches (including a large one on the Central Park West façade proclaiming "Erected 1929") (Figure 135).

At the terraced setbacks the ornamentation gets more profuse, encompassing obelisks, finials, colonnettes, pilasters, corbeled consoles, garlands, angelic cherubs, stark skulls, ram's heads, and still more balustrades, pediments and cartouches (Figure 136).

The grand finale to this stone symphony: the fully orchestrated triple towers. These nearly Baroque exclamation points are enclosed pavilions (the northern one was originally open). All are octagonal, exuberantly ornamented, crowned with œil-de-bœuf windows, topped with Mission tile roofs and surmounted by tall copper lanterns that are lighted at night.

The lobbies are especially distinctive. The two on West 81st Street are modest in size and separate from each other and from the avenue entrance. (The West 82nd Street entry is less important and is connected internally to the Central Park West one.) This contrasts with the more customary arrangement in other large buildings (such as the Century and the Majestic) of a huge, rambling lobby interconnecting all elevator banks. The Beresford's multiple lobbies also lend a more intimate residential scale to a building whose scale can hardly be called intimate. They are lavish, with much marble, ornamental plasterwork and bronze detailing. Adding to the poshness are the elevators, which serve only one or two apartments apiece at each landing.

The units originally ranged from four to 16 rooms, with the majority being "conventional" luxury apartments of eight to ten rooms. (Many have been altered over the years; some were augmented and others reduced). The majority are simplexes, but there are also many duplexes and even some triplexes. Each has a central entrance and circulation gallery, so the otherwise ubiquitous long corridors were unnecessary. This also adds to the grandeur and sense of expansive space within the apartments. Not that they were not spacious to begin with. Living rooms are as large as 20

Figure 134. *The Beresford, giving the impression of a European fortress of the Renaissance when seen from within Central Park, ca. 1950. (Hannau, Galerie St. Etienne.)*

by 36 feet, and some bedrooms measure 18 feet by 28. Ceilings are devoid of beam projections and set at ten feet on the lower floors and a lofty 12 feet at the terraced upper levels.

There is one especially grand apartment with a double-height studio living room in the southeast corner tower and additional rooms on three separate levels below. Home to magazine editor Helen Gurley Brown and her producer-husband David, the apartment was formerly owned by producer-director Mike Nichols. These people are representative of the Beresford tenantry, many of whom are from the arts and entertainment industries. Others have included Isaac Stern, Beverly Sills, Tony Randall, Sheldon Harnick and columnist Leonard Lyons. Anthropologist Margaret Mead also lived there.

Left: Figure 135. *The bulky Beresford Apartments, Central Park West at West 81st Street, ca. 1940. (Courtesy of Christopher Gray.)* Opposite, top: Figure 136. *One of the setback terraces showing the ornamental ironwork and decorative terra-cotta embellishments, ca. 1950. (Courtesy of Christopher Gray.)* Opposite, bottom: Figure 137. *The view that could be enjoyed from a nine-room terraced apartment that sold in 1962 for $40,700. (Courtesy of Christopher Gray.)*

The Beresford was one of the last great apartment buildings to be erected under the old tenement-house law of 1901, which permitted much greater bulk than would the multiple-dwelling law of 1929, which superseded it. It has an overwhelming presence on the skyline and can be instantly identified from the other side of the park. Those kept out of many of the Fifth Avenue buildings could show the world they had arrived even more grandly on Central Park West.

Completed only a month before the stock-market crash of 1929, the building had a hard time fighting off the Great Depression. It succumbed in 1940, and was sold in tandem with the San Remo Apartments for the incredible sum of $25,000 over the mortgages (for *both* buildings). Recovering after World War II, it

went on to become a cooperative in 1962—among the first on Central Park West. One of the nine-room apartments with a terrace was offered then to outsiders for $40,700 *(Figure 137)*. A similar eight-room-plus-terrace unit was put up for sale in 1988 for $3,500,000—a compound interest growth rate of more than 18 percent a year consistently over 26 years. Not too shabby a return on the investment, and proof that the Beresford represents solid, deeply entrenched value. Emery Roth must have realized that enduring value comes from within, as he embellished the armorial shield on the brass elevator doors with the motto *Fronti Nulla Fides,* which translates as "Don't Trust Appearances."

Tuscan Tapestry

Texture and terra-cotta at 898 Park Avenue

FAVORABLE REAL-ESTATE-TAX-ABATEMENT legislation in 1921 gave strong impetus to the creation of multifamily housing in New York. This factor was combined with a rapidly increasing urban population that needed housing, and an expanding social acceptance of apartment living for the money classes. The result was a record of more residential units being created during the 1920s than during any other ten-year period before or since. Present-day reactionary voices railing against high-rise construction and against tax breaks for luxury apartments might well go back and relearn the lesson of the twenties. The buildings erected then were generally much taller than what they replaced, and the tax subsidies applied across the board to rich and poor alike. The beneficial result was a large amount of additional housing stock for the city.

The accommodations met the needs of an exceedingly broad market, encompassing modest units of one or two bedrooms and extending to expansive layouts of several thousand square feet. The majority of these were conceived as rentals, but many were formed as joint ownership, or cooperative, corporations.

The cooperatives were, by and large, architecturally distinct. With very rare exceptions, each builder had profit as his primary objective. In a rental venture, the profit would be prolonged, coming in slowly over the terms of the leases, while the risk would be increased.

But with a cooperative, the builder could sell the individual apartments and take out his profits as soon as he had sold out. With the expectation of financial risk for only two or three years, he could sink more into the quality of the design and construction than he might for a rental. And if he were particularly careful in planning, he might even be able to sell out before construction was completed.

That was what the Mandel-Ehrich Corporation hoped to do. Henry Mandel was an experienced developer and builder: He had erected the Postal Life office building in 1913 at Fifth Avenue and 43rd Street, and the block-long Pershing Square Building at East 42nd Street and Park Avenue. That massive structure on Park Avenue was distinguished by its highly textured brickwork and Northern Italian pre-Renaissance design elements.

Early in 1924, Mandel embarked on a residential project at East 79th Street. Since his Tuscan motifs were successful in his just-completed East 42nd Street office building, he decided to use them for his new apartment house, but on a more intimate and domestic scale.

Mandel's instincts as a builder had always been good, beginning with a two-story commercial building at West 96th Street and Broadway, which he completed when he was only a 20-year-old-independent entrepreneur. His office buildings had been successful, but he wanted a quickly profitable project that would

Opposite: Figure 138. *The textured tower of 898 Park Avenue flanked by lowrise row houses, ca. 1940. The building remains freestanding. (William Henry.)*

Above, left: Figure 139. *The Tuscan-style terra-cotta ornamentation at the entrance to 898 Park Avenue in 1925, before the building was occupied. (R. W. Sexton.)* Above, right: Figure 140. *The entrance as rendered with a fair amount of proportion-changing artistic license for the original sales brochure of 898 Park Avenue. (Collection of Andrew Alpern.)*

allow him to get his money back speedily. A small cooperative apartment house would fit the bill very nicely.

Mandel hired architects John Sloan and Albert E. Nast to design 898 Park Avenue in the Northern Italian style he had found both aesthetically interesting and financially rewarding. (Mandel went on to use the same stylistic elements in the One Park Avenue loft building in 1926, and in the huge London Terrace apartment complex in 1929. And he memorialized the style by erecting two apartment hotels, The Lombardy on East 56th Street in 1927 and The Tuscany on East 39th Street in 1928.)

Having already been given stylistic marching orders by Mandel, architects Sloan and Nast were confronted by the problems of planning a luxury apartment house on a 75-by-41-foot site. Situated on a prominent corner and flanked by low brownstone row houses, it would have to be carefully designed so it would not look out of place. This would not be easy, since it faced an elegant mansion on one corner and a massive 17-story apartment house on another.

The architects designed the building as a simple rectangle—a straight tower without a setback *(Figure 138)*. To emphasize the domestic scale of the structure, they used a yellowish brick laid with a tapestrylike texture and embellished the façade with intricately decorated colonnettes, arches, pilasters, panels and grotesques *(Figures 139 & 140)*. These decorative elements appeared to be carved stone, but were in fact cast terra-cotta, some of them polychromed. This ornamentation, some of which was far from historically Tuscan *(Figure 141)*, was used primarily at the building's entrance and around the ground-floor windows, but also appeared at the fifth-floor and upper-floor belt courses and at the penthouse.

The planning of the individual apartments by Sloan and Nast was also on a domestic scale, albeit a rather grandly gracious one. The entire building originally consisted of six duplex apartments, a single-floor unit at the second floor and a doctor's suite at ground level. The duplexes were more than 5000 square feet apiece, but since they were compactly planned they had the feeling of a private house. (Many comparably sized apartments of the period had a stretched-out-along-a-corridor impression.)

On the lower floor of each duplex was a 36-foot-long living room with windows on three sides, a spacious dining room, a kitchen and four servants' rooms. A large foyer and elegantly elliptical stair led to the five bedrooms and four baths on the upper floor (*Figure 142*). The ceiling heights of almost 11 feet, and the completely hidden columns, beams and radiators—enhanced by appropriate decorative moldings—made each unit seem even larger than it was.

The amenities included working fireplaces in the living rooms and master bedrooms, elaborate bathroom fittings, kitchens with six-burner ranges, and individual laundry rooms in the basement. There were additional servants' quarters on the ground floor and roof, and heat was provided by piped-in steam, obviating the need for a below-grade boiler or coal-storage rooms.

Completed in 1924, 898 Park Avenue offered these

Figure 141. *Some of the ornamental work prior to its installation, photographed at the studios of its fabricator, the Atlantic Terra Cotta Company. The figures, designed to flank the entrance, represent an immigrant laborer, a Dutch burgher, a frontiersman and an Indian brave complete with hunting bow and tomahawak. Hardly Tuscan. (Courtesy of the Atlantic Terra Cotta Company.)*

Figure 142. *A sketch from the original sales brochure showing the elliptical connecting stair within each apartment. (Collection of Andrew Alpern.)*

13-room duplexes at prices ranging from $54,000 to $62,000, with monthly maintenance charges averaging $700. Each of the four elevator men serving the building earned $20 per week, and the total annual labor cost, all-inclusive for the nine service people at the building, was less than $10,000.

That was 1924. Then came the Great Depression and with it the foreclosures that doomed so many of the grand old apartments of the earlier, more prosperous years. Only two of the duplexes of 898 Park Avenue have survived, the rest having been converted in 1948 by architect Simon Zelnick to simplex units— still large, but nowhere near as grand as what had originally been built.

The brownstone on Park Avenue directly to the

south of Number 898, complemented by the row of brownstones along East 79th Street, originally set the apartment house apart from its neighbors as a stark, free-standing tower. The avenue holdout remains, and by a quirk of fate, so does the separation on East 79th Street. A new apartment tower was constructed behind the façades of several of those side-street houses, but the two easterly ones designed in 1884 by James Edward Ware have remained inviolate. The visual distinction of Sloan and Nast's design is thus preserved, and Henry Mandel's affection for a style variously described as Lombardy Romanesque or Tuscan Tapestry is perpetuated in the delight it contributes to the streetscape.

Ersatz English

*A vestigial memory of London on West 23rd Street
and Ninth Avenue*

THE SIGNS SAY "LONDON TERRACE" and the publicity releases proclaim "The Great Briton in Manhattan," yet the buildings hark back to early Tuscan architecture and the traditions of Lombardy. Could the incongruity be nothing more than a marketing ploy to exploit perceptions of English charm?

The reality, in fact, lies in the whim of an old military man more than two centuries ago. Seeking a retirement home, Captain Thomas Clarke bought a large piece of the old Somerindyke farm in 1750 and named it Chelsea, after his native London's Royal Hospital at Chelsea, where old soldiers spend their final years.

About midway between Ninth and Tenth Avenues, just south of what is now West 23rd Street, the captain built a "snug harbor" that he called Chelsea House. By 1776, though, he was bedridden and near death. A fire destroyed his home that year, and soon he was gone too.

But the property stayed in the family. His widow rebuilt the house and defended it against British troops during the Revolutionary War, and remained there until her death in 1802. Her daughter, Charity, inherited the property.

She added it to the holdings of her husband, Benjamin Moore, the Episcopal bishop of New York and president of Columbia College. In 1813, the couple deeded the land and its buildings to their son, Clement Clarke Moore. Although the younger Moore's life stretched from the middle of the Revolutionary War to the middle of the Civil War and included an impressive series of accomplishments, he is best

known for having written, in 1822, the magical poem that begins, "'T was the night before Christmas, when all through the house . . . ."

Clement Moore was also a far-seeing businessman who understood good urban planning and canny real-estate development. With his friend James N. Wells, a local real-estate broker, Moore carefully divided his lands into lots conforming to the new street pattern and sold them for fine residences. To establish suitable neighbors, he donated an entire block to the General Theological Seminary (whose buildings and grounds are redolent of the colleges at Oxford and Cambridge), and gave land on West 20th Street to St. Peter's Episcopal Church for a rectory and a sanctuary.

He then began a major development project encompassing the block from West 23rd to 24th streets and Ninth to Tenth Avenues. On the shady West 24th Street frontage he built the Chelsea Cottages: wood-framed two-story houses for working people. The entire West 23rd Street frontage was improved with 36 grand brownstone row houses, all set well back from the pavement behind hedges and trees *(Figure 143)*. Each dwelling was designed in the popular Greek Revival style, creating a uniform vista of three-storied pilasters and recessed spandrels with Greek-key carving. Completed in 1845, the development was called London Terrace, expanding on the English allusion first expounded by Captain Clarke almost a century before.

Moore insisted on high-quality constructions, raising the value of his remaining property. Recognizing this, he razed the family seat across from London

Terrace in 1853 and sold the land *(Figure 144)*. On the site, elaborate row houses were built in the flamboyant Anglo-Italianate style. Facing the then-still-new London Terrace, these later houses quickly earned the sobriquet "Millionaires' Row."

Moore died in 1863, but because of the complexities of his real-estate holdings, his estate was not settled until 1907. That was a year of financial panic (what we might today call a serious recession), which marked the beginning of the original London Terrace's decline.

In the following years, what had been expensive one-family homes were subdivided into rooming houses and apartments. Extra floors were added to several of the buildings, and some were thrown together as institutions. Three midblock houses formed the Agnes Cloud Residence, while three more near Tenth Avenue were combined with a trio of the West 24th Street cottages to form the School for Social Research "campus" *(Figure 145)*.

As the buildings decined, however, the land value

Opposite, top: Figure 143. *The original London Terrace, as developed by Clement Clarke Moore in 1845, ca. 1900. (Courtesy of The New-York Historical Society.)* Opposite, bottom: Figure 144. *The eighteenth-century house built by Thomas Clarke's widow on the ruins of the old captain's original Chelsea House, as it appeared around 1850, not long before it was razed. (Nathaniel Fish Moore, courtesy of the Museum of the City of New York.)* Below: Figure 145. *The first London Terrace, shortly before demolition, looking east from Tenth Avenue. (Courtesy of Consolidated Edison Company.)*

Figure 146. *An early, unrealized scheme for Henry Mandel's London Terrace apartment-house project. (Collection of Andrew Alpern.)*

rose. Developer Henry Mandel recognized this and gradually acquired control of the block. By 1929 he had it all, at least on paper. Gaining actual possession, though, proved more difficult. He had not reckoned on Tillie Hart.

Hart lived at 429 West 23rd Street on a sublease that, she asserted, was valid until May 1930. The underlying prime lease had already expired, however, giving Mandel the legal right of possession. But Hart steadfastly refused to move, despite the demolition going on around her.

By October 1929, Mandel had demolished all the existing structures except Hart's. Her increasingly histrionic tactics were duly reported in the newspapers, with her lawyers delaying the matter in court while she barricaded herself in, and pelted any would-be intruders with bricks and stones. The sheriffs managed to enter on October 25, however, and placed

all Hart's belongings on the front pavement. Obstinate to the last, she spent that night in the house sleeping on newspapers spread out on the floor. The following day she finally abandoned the fight, and the wreckers demolished the house in short order.

Mandel, the spiritual forebear of the flamboyant builders of today, had recently completed two hotels and his luxury Park Avenue cooperative building. For his newly vacant block, he had decided to erect what was to be the largest apartment house New York City had ever seen.

Mandel hired the architectural firm of Farrar & Watmough, a partnership formed in 1925 by Victor Farrar and Richard Watmough. Pleased with the round-arched and highly ornamental Tuscan style he had used repeatedly before, Mandel instructed the architects to use it for the new project.

An early scheme called for 12 buildings of 16 stories each along West 23rd and 24th streets, with a single cross-shaped tower rising more than twice the height of the rest at Ninth Avenue. The landscaped center was to be protected on the Tenth Avenue side by a modest two-story structure *(Figure 146)*.

The later plan, which was eventually realized, comprised ten midblock buildings with taller and bulkier structures at all four corners. The inner court was foreshortened to allow for a large, enclosed swimming pool at the Tenth Avenue end and an equally large restaurant at the other. The design was accepted by the city's Department of Buildings under the old tenement-house law of 1901. (With the more urbanistically sensitive multiple-dwelling law of 1929, the structures would not have been permitted to rise so high without setbacks.)

Mandel's project was completed in two phases, with the ten smaller buildings finished in 1930 and the four corner towers constructed the following year. Despite its distinctively Southern Italian design and detailing, the complex picked up the old name, London Terrace. Professor Moore himself was remembered at the cornerstone-laying ceremony, with his 15-year-old great-great-grandson doing the honors with the trowel. It was even asserted at the time that the cornerstone itself had come from the Moore's family manse, Chelsea House (unlikely, since that building had been demolished some 66 years earlier).

The buildings contained, within a single block, an astounding 1665 apartments. Most were either studios or one-bedrooms, with only a few larger apartments in the corner buildings and at the terraced levels. With more than 4000 residential rooms, the density was vastly more than the worst slums of Calcutta *(Figure 147)*.

Yet London Terrace's special amenities were attractive: a 75-by-35-foot indoor swimming pool with balconied viewing galleries and adjoining locker rooms; a

Figure 147. *The completed London Terrace in 1932—14 buildings; 1665 apartments; 4000+ rooms. (Wurts Brothers, courtesy of the Museum of the City of New York.)*

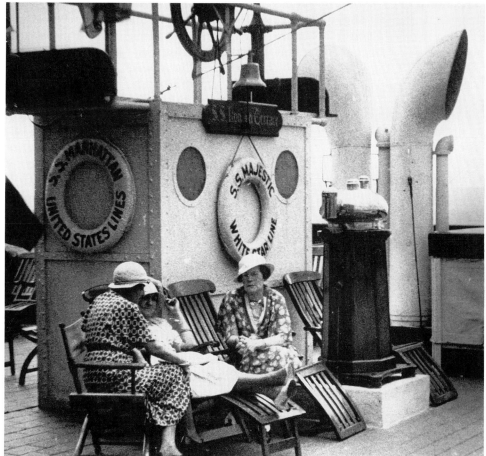

Figure 148. *Aboard the good ship S.S.* London Terrace: *the rooftop sun deck at the Tenth Avenue end of the project, ca. 1935. (Courtesy of The New-York Historical Society.)*

Figure 149. *The entrance to the renting office, ca. 1930, was through the lobby of one of the buildings of London Terrace. (Irving Browning, courtesy of The New-York Historical Society.)*

supervised rooftop play area for children; an equipped gymnasium; a penthouse recreational club; a sun deck for infants; a courtyard garden; and a marine deck fitted out and furnished as if it were part of a great ocean liner. Set 21 stories above the street, this last element allowed residents to look down on the real-life ships that docked a few blocks away *(Figure 148)*.

Besides ready access to the on-site shops and services via the internal tunnels that connected the entire complex, residents could use an array of free services including: page boys for delivering messages within the complex or running nearby errands; a telephone-message-receiving service that would bring the message slips to the apartments; and a mail-and-package room that would deliver to the apartments on call.

Topping the list of tenants who enjoyed these services were secretaries (202 of them), as well as engineers, attorneys, accountants and "presidents of companies." They paid an average of $30 monthly rent per room *(Figure 149)*.

That seemingly low rate was possible only through imaginative marketing and "selectivity" in management. According to a contemporary report by the renting agent, William A. White & Sons, "Restrictions are especially important in London Terrace . . . [and] a careful check of business, social and financial references is made before leases are signed." Notwithstanding that care, the Great Depression, which struck

just as London Terrace was being completed, forced developer Mandel into personal bankruptcy in 1932 and precipitated foreclosure in 1934. A magazine article early in that year described this nightmarish financial morass, noting that "nobody is clear as to who owns what and what what is worth."

The claims, counterlcaims and changes in title went on until 1945, when the ownership of the original ten buildings and the four corner towers was split. London Terrace Gardens (the inner buildings) continued as a rental. London Terrace Towers was eventually converted to a combination condominium–co-op (a condop). Under this scheme, a one-bedroom apartment that once rented for $90 a month was offered in 1988 for $150,000 to buy, with a monthly carrying charge of $725. Taking into account what most New Yorkers earned in the 1930s, the relative cost of that apartment probably has not changed all that much.

The four converted and renovated buildings are now called The Towers at London Terrace, and are marketed as "The Great Briton in Manhattan." With advertisements featuring period photographs of Henry Mandel's original doormen dressed as London "bobbies" (shades of Trump Tower's original busby-hatted door attendants) and the emphasis on England in the promotional efforts, it would appear that the perceptions of English charm have remained constant over the intervening years. Old Captain Thomas Clarke would have been proud.

Riverfront Refuge

Exclusive enclave at 435 East 52nd Street

AS THE WORLD SLID into the depths of the Great Depression, many New Yorkers found themselves in a battle each day merely to put food on the table. Others were forced to abandon their large apartments on Park and Fifth avenues and seek more modest quarters. But not all the lights were dimmed.

Builder James Stewart recognized that some city dwellers were financially insulated from the chilling effects of the economic depression. He also saw the potential of a spectacular 40,000-square-foot property fronting directly on that tidal estuary called the East River.

William L. Bottomley of the architectural firm of Bottomley, Wagner & White was retained to develop that potential as a huge cooperative apartment house. He faced some serious challenges to his ingenuity. The city had recently enacted a new multiple-dwelling law and the new project would be the first on the river to come within its purview. Many aspects of the new law appeared to conflict with Bottomley's plan, and he had to negotiate long and hard with the Department of Buildings to obtain final approval of the project's construction drawings.

The site, which extended from East 52nd to 53rd Streets along the East River, was an even greater challenge. Property lines were clear enough, but construction limits at the river's edge were ambiguous; different recorded maps showed different high-water lines. In addition, each of the two side streets was a dead end, posing potential traffic problems, and the 30-foot drop from the southern to the northern boundary made planning especially difficult.

Bottomley made assets of these liabilities. He solved the dead-end problems by creating a spacious court-yard at the westerly side *(Figure 150)*. This *cour d'honneur* was raised to the East 52nd Street level and connected by a ramp to 53rd. The architect embellished it with bushes, trees and fountains, and designed a grand entrance gate facing south *(Figure 151)*. He placed a second, more private, courtyard on the river side, giving it an ornamental fountain as well *(Figure 152)*.

The space beneath the courtyard was "landlocked," and the lower portion of the remainder of the site could have northern and eastern windows only. Because this severely limited its ability to accommodate apartment units, the architect proposed to use the space for a private club. To do that, he needed special permission from the various regulatory city agencies. He obtained it. The apartment house was to be called River House, so its social and recreational adjunct was named The River Club. The club consumed not only the three floors beneath the courtyard entrance, but also most of the two above. Excepted was the entrance lobby *(Figure 153),* and a space carved out for a spacious triplex maisonette apartment for Bottomley himself. This had a private entrance and small office opening directly off the entrance courtyard. The River Club included the customary drawing room, dining room and ballroom, as well as a bar and bedrooms. It also boasted a gymnasium, a swimming pool and two tennis courts. Its special distinction, however, was the private marina and yacht landing *(Figure 154)*.

Above the club rose River House itself. It comprised two 15-story wings and a 27-story central tower *(Figure 155)*. Simplex and duplex units of nine to 17

Right: Figure 150. *The courtyard entrance to River House, ca. 1931. The door at the left led to the triplex maisonette apartment of the building's architect. (Gottscho-Schleisner, courtesy of the Museum of the City of New York.)* Below: Figure 151. *The windowed sentry box and gates guarding the entrance courtyard of River House, ca. 1931. (Gottscho-Schleisner, courtesy of the Museum of the City of New York.)*

rooms were nothing short of magnificent. Crowning the tower was a 17-room triplex boasting multiple terraces, a private elevator and a palatial drawing room 46 feet long and 22 feet high.

A more "typical" 13-room simplex including four bedrooms, four maids' rooms and a 65-foot *enfilade* of drawing room, library and dining room, all along the water. Each apartment offered a river view, and many had loggias, balconies or terraces, as well.

In 1931, the tower triplex carried a price tag of $275,000 (100 times the annual salary of an experienced CPA) and the least expensive unit cost $37,000. That may sound low by today's standards, but when River House opened, only the particularly wealthy could buy. Those first residents included Cornelius Vanderbilt Whitney, Marshall Field III and Ruth Baker Pratt, widow of a Standard Oil Company founder's son. Others were William Rhinelander Stewart, Jr., a flamboyant and handsome man-about-town; Edwin Armstrong, of radio fame; and socialites Harry Cushing and James A. Burden, Jr. In later years River House was home to violinist-composer Fritz Kreisler, actress Dina Merrill (whose mother was Mrs. E. F. Hutton), retailer Walter Hoving, Joshua Logan and a German-Jewish immigrant named Henry Kissinger.

The River Club serves a number of upstairs residents, but its membership of more than 700 now includes five Rockefellers, a prince and a princess. At its opening, the rolls featured six Whitneys, three Vanderbilts, three Iselins, seven Pratts, four Burdens and two Cuttings. It was (and is) one of the most socially elite family clubs in the city.

The formidable barriers to membership (including a five-year waiting list) are more than matched by the difficulties of gaining acceptance in River House itself. Most cooperatives carefully screen potential purchasers, but the board of directors at this one is especially vigilant in maintaining standards. A "name" and a few million dollars are not necessarily sufficient.

One such hapless applicant was the much-married Gloria Vanderbilt. In 1980, she sought a quiet home in which she could escape the pain of the outside world. Seeking to purchase a tower duplex at River House,

Figure 152. *A photograph ca. 1931, showing the architect's own living room, which overlooked this east-facing courtyard fountain. (Gottscho-Schleisner, courtesy of the Museum of the City of New York.)*

Above, top: Figure 153. *One portion of the lobby of River House, ca. 1931. (Gottscho-Schleisner, courtesy of the Museum of the City of New York.)* Above, bottom: Figure 154. *The private boat landing directly on the East River, ca. 1931. It was destroyed when the FDR Drive was constructed. (Gottscho-Schleisner, courtesy of the Museum of the City of New York.)*

Figure 155. *River House before the East River Drive partially obscured it, seen from what is now Roosevelt Island, ca. 1931.* *(Courtesy of the Museum of the City of New York.)*

she was rejected even before she could appear in front of the board members. The apartment price was $1.1 million, which Vanderbilt offered to place in escrow. Yet her ability to handle the expense was not the problem. The board asserted that her presence would bring "unwelcome publicity" to the building. Seemingly to prove that point, she brought a lawsuit against the board. She charged that it was discriminating against her because of her sex and her very close friendship with black musician Bobby Short.

Vanderbilt never did get to live in River House, even though her cousin, Harold S. Vanderbilt (pre-

eminent yachtsman and inventor of contract bridge), was an original and longtime resident. She "settled" for an expansive terraced duplex at 10 Gracie Square, a building that also fronts on the East River and, similarly, is one of the few in the city to have a through-the-block entrance driveway.

The apartment Vanderbilt had tried to buy was the lower two floors of what had originally been the $275,000 tower triplex. That spectacular aerie had lasted only until 1938, when it was subdivided into a lower duplex incorporating the double-height drawing room of the original apartment, and an upper unit.

Forty years later, the upper apartment was bought (reportedly for $260,000) by lawyer and financier Robert Postel and his wife Joan. When the Vanderbilt skirmish was resolved and the lower duplex put back on the market, it was purchased by Salomon Brothers chairman John Gutfreund and his wife Susan. The board may have wished in retrospect that it had accepted Vanderbilt, because the fireworks from the clash of Joan Postel and Susan Gutfreund brought more notoriety than anyone could have imagined. Even the previously rejected Richard Nixon probably would not have generated as much negative publicity.

Susan Gutfreund's husband had gained many millions of dollars from the Phibro Corporation's acquisition of Salomon Brothers, and she spent a goodly chunk of it reconstructing and redecorating her newly acquired apartment.

The 1938 division of the original triplex had given the private elevator over to the upper unit for access, but both apartments had to share the twenty-fourth-floor landing and vestibule. Susan Gutfreund's forceful personality and renovation work brought her into conflict with Joan Postel, her upstairs neighbor. The antagonism came to a head at Christmas in 1982, when Gutfreund bought a 22-foot-high, 14-foot-diameter, 500-pound Douglas fir as a Christmas tree. It was more than the building's elevator or tower stairs could handle. The only possibility was to hoist it up the outside using a rig anchored to the building's top. Postel thought otherwise, refusing to permit Gutfreund's men to set up on "her" roof.

The Postels were renovating their own apartment, and this presented an opportunity. Disguised as a Postel workman, one of the Gutfreund riggers gained access to the upper apartment and opened the stair door to his fellow workers. They went out onto the roof, quickly hoisted the huge tree to the Gutfreunds' floor, and swung it in through an opening made available by the removal of a drawing-room window. Mission accomplished, they retreated, later submitting a bill of more than $3000 for installing the $500 seasonal ornament.

The tale did not end there. The Postels brought a lawsuit against the Gutfreunds, charging them with "willful, malicious, wrongful, and otherwise corrupt activities" and several other choice accusations, including that they imprisoned the young Postel son in the building's elevator and subjected him to verbal abuse. The Postels also sued the River House board, saying that the members should not have permitted the Christmas operation to take place.

To help prove that neither the board nor the Gutfreunds had any right to use the tower roof for tree hoisting, the Postels hired architecture historian Christopher Gray, who searched the Department of Buildings' records and found that the original architects had altered their own plans. Before construction had been completed, they had turned the original triplex into a quadruplex. A service space at the very top of the building was turned into a reception room with French doors opening onto the roof, which had become an "observation deck." Private stairs made this extra amenity readily accessible from the triplex. When the grand apartment was cut up in 1938, the reception room and observation deck went with the upper apartment, which thereby qualified as a duplex.

Armed with Gray's findings, the Postels charged into battle. The Gutfreunds, however, retreated. John Gutfreund bought a $6.5-million apartment at 834 Fifth Avenue and the couple moved out of the ill-fated River House duplex. Ironically, their architect retained Gray to research the Department of Buildings' records for their new apartment, perhaps in an attempt to avoid a replay.

River House residents have generally maintained their apartments as homes of refuge and retreat from the prying eyes of lesser mortals. History seems to be proving, though, that the rarified heights of luxurious riverfront living bring with them a propensity for aggressive behavior and the scrutiny of an inquisitive public. It's awfully hard to be invisible when you're rich and famous.

Depression Deco

A practical response to an altered economy at
25 Central Park West

IN THE WAKE OF the 1929 stock-market crash, a financial malaise spread, and family after family was forced to retrench. Each sought a practical way of dealing with a drastically altered economy.

Veteran real-estate entrepreneur Irwin S. Chanin evaluated the problem and measured it against a large piece of property he had acquired not long before the crash. This land, the entire block bounded by West 62nd and 63rd Streets, and by Central Park West and Broadway, did not have a long history of development. As late as 1902, it was the only block remaining along Central Park West that was still undeveloped (except for a few tiny one-story frame structures). Because the neighborhood abounded in showrooms and garages catering to the newfangled but rapidly accepted automobile, similar buildings began to appear at the westerly end of the block. The remainder contained a small studio building of the same period and a modest church that later became Daly's Theatre.

In 1908, the Central Park West frontage was acquired for a subsidized civic repertory theater. Designed by the eminent architectural firm of Carrère & Hastings (working concurrently on the new Public Library at Fifth Avenue and West 42nd Street), the New Theatre opened on November 8, 1909 with a performance of *Antony and Cleopatra*. The noble experiment of repertory lasted only two seasons, however, and the building then became a conventional Broadway house called the Century Theatre. It served as a venue for large-scale musicals and spectaculars, and even enjoyed a brief fling as an opera house *(Figure 156)*.

The Shubert organization bought the Century Theatre in 1920, but had limited success; it was too far from the Times Square theater district. Irwin Chanin, who had built and retained partial ownership of the Royale, Masque and Majestic Theatres, struck a deal with the Shuberts: he exchanged those successful houses for the larger but less profitable Century.

In August 1929, Chanin announced the redevelopment project: a 65-story skyscraper would be erected on the full-block site. This French-American effort was to be called the Palais de France. Billed as the French commercial capital in America, it would have three floors of display space for French goods and materials, and a 27-story hotel. The top 30 stories would be office space for the French consulate and tourist board and French companies.

The design was the new avant-garde style known as Art Deco, and plans were to make extensive use of French glass blocks and a new form of plate glass. Six French sculptors were to be brought over to work on the structure.

The plan was grand, and it might have come off if not for the disaster on Wall Street a little more than two months later, and the economic depression that followed. As it was, Chanin went to France with his American banker to secure financing, but returned empty-handed.

Forced to abandon the Palais de France for lack of funds and lack of occupancy commitments, Chanin reevaluated the site and his plans. By the autumn of 1930, the Depression had deepened, and more families were unable to maintain large apartments. Chanin

Figure 156. *The Century Theatre, shown in 1910, obtained by Irwin Chanin through a trade with the Shubert organization. (Ewing Galloway, courtesy of Irwin S. Chanin.)*

sensed that he could meet the growing need for smaller dwelling units by offering amenities in place of space. He was registered as an architect early in 1930, and followed not long after with an announcement that he would erect a huge, twin-towered Art Deco apartment house on the site of the Century Theatre.

Seeking to reach a market that wanted pre-Depression luxury but could only afford smaller space, Chanin planned the new building accordingly. He knew he would have to offer features of the largest old apartments, but with fewer and smaller rooms. Also sensitive to the emotional trauma of trading down, he sought to provide an exceptionally large variety of units, which added the luxury of choice. And, finally, he realized that a significant spatial change was more palatable if accompanied by a dramatic aesthetic one as

well. His new building would be in the Art Deco style *(Figure 157)*.

The Art Deco building was a dynamic shift from the conventional, Classical apartment houses built until then. The façades of most had Corinthian pilasters, Roman pediments, bracketed cornices and balustraded balconies. Inside, there was paneling, elaborate moldings, grand fireplace mantels and decorative detailing by the running mile. Anything less than large, elegantly Classical furniture would look out of place.

But within the simplified and smaller Art Deco units, simpler, smaller and less expensive furniture would be appropriate. Simpler living—without a crew of servants—would be more acceptable. The new design motifs were more than an arbitrary decoration; they helped cushion the shock of the Great Depression.

Chanin planned the apartments (as noted in one of

Figure 157. *The Depression-era Art Deco-style Century Apartments, 1931. (Wurts Brothers, courtesy of Irwin S. Chanin.)*

the original rental brochures) as "small and moderate-sized homes in which beauty, comfort, and pride of possession are added to the engineering and scientific achievements of those who have had a part in their plan and construction."

The original drawings called for 416 apartments of 52 distinct varieties, ranging from a single room with a small serving pantry to an 11-room duplex maisonette with a private entrance from the street. Almost any could include a terrace: A small one-room apartment with a boudoir and a pantry could have one with two exposures.

To have a terrace in Manhattan with anything but a very large apartment was quite unusual. Even more uncommon and, perhaps, unique, were the one-bedroom duplex apartments. These gave the impression of grand and gracious space spread over two separate floors—yet all within the modest confines of only three rooms.

This unit could be left plain, or could include a guest lavatory, a dining alcove, a living room dropped two steps below the foyer, a terrace or almost any combination of these extras.

A particularly unusual and attractive amenity was a corner solarium with a special glass that let in the sun's ultraviolet light for indoor winter sun-tanning. During the summer, the solarium could be fitted with insect screens for use as a sleeping porch. Solaria were available with four-, five-, six- or seven-room apartments, in most cases paired with dropped living rooms.

The original lobby decoration was a stripped-down, American version of the more elaborate French Art Deco style. Most of the architectural features are still there, but the clunky furniture upholstered in bold geometric fabrics deteriorated over the years and was discarded. Some minimal redecoration and refurbishing has been done in recent years, but the vast lobby remains grim and underfurnished. There were six manned elevator banks. The labyrinthine, U-shaped lobby had ground-floor entrances on West 62nd and 63rd Streets and Central Park West. Each had (and still has) two 24-hour attendants.

Irwin Chanin's Century Apartments opened at 25 Central Park West as a rental, and remained that way long after most other buildings on that avenue became cooperatives. For years it was well maintained, but the limitations of the "temporary" wartime rent controls reduced the cash-flow increases that were needed to meet rising costs. Services declined, paving the way for a conversion.

This was attempted in 1983, but tenants repelled it, vainly seeking to have a city administrator appointed as manager. This tactic was often employed with deteriorating slum buildings. The tenants' lawyer claimed that the Century had indeed achieved slum status, but the court rejected his argument. The state attorney general's office then derailed the conversion plan because the sponsors had omitted from the prospectus the 140 violations pending against the building. They had also refrained from disclosing the possibility of significant tax increases following the conversion and they did not reveal certain important financial information about themselves.

In 1987, a new conversion prospectus was filed, this time as a condominium. To ensure that the earlier battles would not recur, tenants were offered some unusual concessions, and purchasing residents were given a 37 percent discount.

Outside buyers paid more, but they did not get more. Outsiders ordinarily are offered new kitchens, yet in the Century conversion they got none at all. The sponsor had removed all fixtures, cabinets and appliances from the vacant units, and sold the space with only the existing plumbing pipes protruding from the bare walls. The assumption was that each buyer would want to install a completely new kitchen to suit personal tastes. The original bathrooms remained, however, although they were not restored or upgraded.

Chanin designed the Century for 1931 occupancy by people seeking modest but pleasant apartments at realistic rents. He recognized the financial constraints of the time. Living to 96 years of age, and seeing the condominium conversion, Chanin may have wondered what happened to his humane (yet profitable) concept: 1987 condominium offering prices exceeded $500,000 for a *one*-bedroom apartment.

Majestic Moderne

Twin-towered testament to zigzags and zoning at
115 Central Park West

THE ONSET OF THE Great Depression forced Irwin Chanin to alter his original plans for the site of what is now the Century Apartments, and it required a comparable change in the project he had announced for 11 blocks further north on Central Park West.

Three elements determine the appearance of all structures in New York: law, economics and aesthetics—in that order. In the first category, the laws are many. Zoning controls dictate where a stable, factory or apartment house can be built. They also determine a building's maximum height and specify how light and air must reach the street. Fire- and highway-department regulations also affect building designs, as do the various housing, plumbing, electrical and general building codes.

Maintaining an even stronger hold over the city's physical development are the "laws" of economics. Seldom are buildings erected without any regard to initial cost, maintenance bills or the "value" received in exchange for the outlay.

Unless the law permits it and the economic conditions are favorable, a building simply will not be built. Only when the first two factors are satisfied does the question of aesthetics arise. While law and economics affect the general appearance of a building, the architect's design determines the style and feel of the finished product.

The massive Majestic Apartments at 115 Central Park West is an excellent example of law, economics and aesthetics at work. Originally the block-long site at the southern corner of West 72nd Street, as shown in the newspapers in 1884 (when the great Dakota apartment house opened across the street), housed nothing more than some ancient wooden shanties and grazing goats. Less than ten years later, however, it was occupied by Alfred Zucker's 12-story Hotel Majestic *(Figure 158)*. Then the latest word in luxurious accommodations, the hotel served both well-heeled transient visitors and socially self-conscious families. The latter were the type that did not want the bother of maintaining a complete brownstone row house, but were not yet willing to accept the "tenement living" of apartment houses.

John Jacob Astor made hotel living acceptable in 1836, the year he opened his large and luxurious Astor House on lower Broadway, just to the north of St. Paul's Chapel. Until 1870, such hotels were the only "proper" alternative to a one-family house. Even after the "French flats" were introduced to New York, hotels remained more desirable for "socially sensitive" folk. Interspersed with the smaller apartment houses going up along Central Park West in the 1890s were large "family" hotels: the El Dorado, the Beresford and the San Remo. All have since been replaced by even larger apartment houses that preserve the names.

The Hotel Majestic was the most southerly of those nineteenth-century hostelries, and by far the most "majestic" and well patronized. Among the guests at various times were Sarah Bernhardt, Gustav Mahler, Sigmund Romberg, Edna Ferber, Pavlova and Nijinsky.

By 1929, however, the 35-year-old hotel was long past its prime. On April 29, 1929, the Chanin Construction Company announced that it intended to

Figure 158. *The Hotel Majestic in its final construction stage, 1894. The sign of the first section of the old Hotel San Remo can be seen in the distance and the site of 101 Central Park West is still an almost-vacant lot. (Courtesy of The New-York Historical Society.)*

build a 45-story, $16-million apartment hotel on the site. The expected completion date was October 1, 1930. The spectacular single-towered structure would offer two distinct classes of accommodations—half conventional apartments with six to 14 rooms in maisonette, simplex and duplex arrangements, and half kitchenette units of one to five rooms. All promised full hotel services, and the building would feature a large central dining room, a grand ballroom and other public spaces. Attitudes were different in those days; no one complained that the old building was a landmark that ought to be preserved, and no one thought the new structure too big for the neighborhood. It was instead recognized as a significant example of modern architecture and necessary real-estate development progress.

Accordingly, the old hotel was demolished. Adjoining row houses on the side streets were also torn down. This yielded a site of 42,000 square feet—a considerable plot of land. Excavations were made, foundations constructed and the supporting steel framework begun. But when the stock market crashed in October 1929, developer Irwin Chanin halted the

work and reevaluated his design. The economic factor then reentered the picture, changing the project from an apartment-hotel into a straight apartment house. In July 1930, Chanin filed new plans to use the existing foundations and steelwork to build a 29-story twin-towered structure rather than the originally intended 45-story single-towered one.

With the redesign came a new wrinkle. In 1929, a new multiple-dwelling law replaced the old tenement-house law of 1901, and the new Majestic apartment house had to conform. The new regulation mandated increased side- and inner-court areas. On sites as large as the Majestic's, however, it allowed for towers that could rise three times the street width. The remainder, though, was restricted in height to 1½ times that width.

Then there was the question of aesthetics. Until that time, apartment houses had been built in various historical styles. These conservative designs were perceived to be residential, while the international Bauhaus and French Art Deco modes were restricted to commercial structures and one-family homes for those with educated and sophisticated tastes.

Figure 159. *The Majestic Apartments in 1931, as redesigned following the stock-market crash of 1929. (Wurts Brothers, courtesy of Irwin S. Chanin.)*

Irwin Chanin, through his in-house architectural designer, Jacques Delamarre, and his decorative expert, sculptor René Chambellan, decided to be aggressively different. He chose a stripped-down Art Deco version that he called Modern American, but which was often referred to as Zigzag Moderne.

This had been an integral part of the earlier 45-story hotel, and was modified and used as well on the successor 29-story apartment house. Unlike the historical styles, which had a horizontal emphasis and a cornice to "end" the building at the roofline, Moderne was vertically oriented. The Majestic's terraced setbacks and twin towers encouraged this sort of scheme (*Figure 159*).

In subtle counterpoint to the new building's verticality were the horizontal cantilevered terraces and strips of windows at the corners. The windows extended the full length of two walls of the corner apartments' solaria. A technically advanced construction method obviated the need for corner columns in the solaria, thereby increasing their sunny openness. The Moderne style permitted these distinctive corner rooms—more traditional forms would have required at least the appearance of heavy masonry piers at the corners. The Moderne aesthetic also allowed a three-part window instead of the conventional double-hung type. The lower section of this new model was an in-swinging hopper that let in a modest amount of air and deflected rain or snow. The middle section was an out-swinging casement, and the fixed upper pane of glass let in light while protecting the pelmets (valances that covered the curtain tops).

While aesthetics affected the interior design, the real driving force was the economic imperative to provide apartments with a competitive advantage. The ultimate goal, after all, was to rent out the apartments, carry the building's costs and make an acceptable profit on the original investment.

Apartments ranged from three to 14 rooms. Some were duplexes, others had terraces and a few even combined the two features. Many had sunken living rooms, and the corner units offered the glazed solaria. There was also a large solarium for the general use of all the tenants, and plans called for a food-service operation as well as valet and maid service.

Particularly careful attention was given to arrangements and fittings. Most units were planned around a central foyer or gallery. In the smallest units, these center halls were of a size we would consider adequate for a decent bedroom today. Those in the largest would now be considered unusually spacious as living rooms.

The large drawing rooms were supplied with working fireplaces, and master bathrooms had separate stall showers, dressing boudoirs, built-in hampers and multiple mirrors. Kitchens were provided with extensive cabinetry, ceramic-tiled walls and the latest in appliances. Floors were of black walnut in the entertaining rooms, and less exotic wood in the remainder. All were set in a plastic cement that eliminated the warping and creaking endemic to the more traditional installation methods. Stock-market crash or not, the apartments at the Majestic were clearly designed to appeal to a moneyed market.

The building opened for occupancy in the autumn of 1931. Irwin Chanin was exceedingly optimistic in his public pronouncements and predictions while he attempted to fill his apartment house. Even as it opened, he told of what he saw as its successor structure—sometime in the next century. In a prediction not unlike some Donald Trump has made, he said the site would be enlarged to accommodate a 2000-foot-high apartment house for 25,000 tenants. He predicted a return to the nineteenth-century mode of apartment-hotel living, with central kitchens and only serving pantries in the apartments.

He also said that "if the new Majestic is in existence after 1981, it will be something of an architectural curiosity. By 1981, I expect the zoning laws under which the new Majestic was built to have been repealed, because they will have outlived their function. The basic purpose of these laws is to insure sunlight and fresh air in a greater supply to every building and to every apartment in each building. Fifty years hence, science and engineering will supply fresh air and sunshine more dependably and more efficiently than nature." He also predicted that in the 1980s we would regularly commute by air at 500 miles per hour. Living to age 96, Irwin Chanin saw it happen.

Even though his predictions may have been accurate, he did not foresee the deep depression that would envelop the country even as he sought tenants for his new structure. He had been given a total consolidated first mortgage of $9.4 million, on which he defaulted in March 1933.

According to historian Peter Salwen, the Majestic had its share of human notoriety on top of its financial problems. Bruno Richard Hauptmann, convicted kidnapper of the Lindbergh baby, worked as a carpenter in the building at the time of the crime. Controversial and déclassé journalist and commentator Walter Winchell lived there, as did crime boss Frank Costello, who was shot in the head in 1957 while walking through the building's lobby.

Although it began as a rental structure, and has had more than its share of difficulties, the Majestic is now a cooperative and enjoys a life of quiet upper-middle-class gentility.

Modified Mansion

*Pulitzer's palace at 11 East 73rd Street becomes
layered luxury lodgings*

IN 1804, LONDON'S MELBOURNE House was converted into apartments that were designed to benefit from the spacious rooms and elegant decoration of that grand mansion. The apartments of Albany in Piccadilly emerged from the white elephant that had been built in 1771 and was later owned by the Duke of York and Albany. Thirty-three years after its construction began, this huge private mansion in London was modified for multifamily living.

Albany proved to be a viable economic concept, and it demonstrated the validity of residential recycling. More than a century later, history repeated itself in New York when, 33 years after the construction of Joseph Pulitzer's East 73rd Street mansion was begun, it too was modified to become a multiple dwelling.

The house was built as the pinnacle of lavish living by one of the most dynamic and successful journalists New York has ever known. Joseph Pulitzer built an immensely influential newspaper empire whose profits endowed the School of Journalism at Columbia University. The Pulitzer Fountain at Fifth Avenue and West 59th Street is one of New York's more elegant adornments and the annual Pulitzer Prizes are another of the man's creative benefactions.

Pulitzer was born in Hungary in 1847, coming to America to seek his fortune. He fought briefly in the Civil War, later becoming active in Missouri state politics. With the profits of a business transaction, he studied law, and was admitted to the bar in 1876. Two years later he took both a wife and an even more demanding mistress, a newspaper.

Pulitzer bought the *St. Louis Dispatch,* orchestrated a merger with the *St. Louis Post,* and within a year had full ownership and control of the joint *St. Louis Post-Dispatch.*

The venture was so successful that only four years later, in 1883, Pulitzer bought the then-sleepy *New York World* from the financier Jay Gould for $346,000. He immediately began his personal revolution against the stodgy journalism of the day, gaining instant publicity for his unorthodox tactics and editorials, and achieving a meteoric rise in circulation. Among the ways he devised to call attention to his paper, and thus to assure its sale each day to an increasing number of New Yorkers, was his public solicitation of funds for the base of the Statue of Liberty. His efforts brought in enough money to construct Richard Morris Hunt's lofty pedestal and, through improved circulation for his newspaper, filled Pulitzer's coffers as well. His fertile brain continually invented new ways of attracting readers. He did massive battle with William Randolph Hearst over which of them could more rapidly precipitate the Spanish–American War, and he introduced the cartoon series "The Yellow Kid," which gave birth to the expression "yellow journalism."

Perhaps exacerbated by his self-imposed work pressures, Pulitzer's weakening health became an increasing burden. His eyesight failed him almost

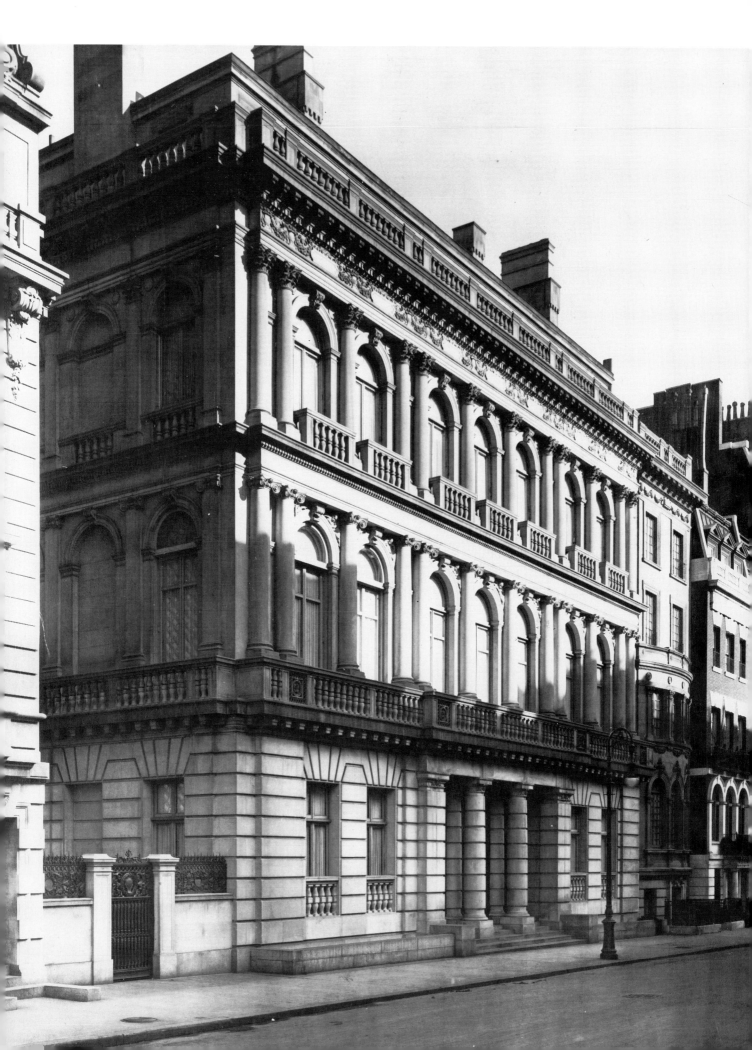

completely, and his nervousness made him inordinately sensitive to noise. Eventually, he had to give up the editorship and daily control of the *World.*

Pulitzer made extensive use of his huge boat, the *Liberty,* but felt that neither that ocean-going yacht nor his relatively modest 33-foot-wide row house was an adequate place to hold court. The house, at 10 East 55th Street, had been designed in 1882 for Charles Tracy Barney by the architectural firm of McKim, Mead & White. That firm altered the house when Pulitzer bought it in 1891, and altered it again in 1894. The issue of a new residence was brought to a head quite dramatically in January 1900, when a fire destroyed the old house, taking the lives of two household servants in the process.

Pulitzer hurriedly purchased a 98-foot-wide piece of property at 11 East 73rd Street just east of Fifth Avenue. He again retained McKim, Mead & White, and persuaded Stanford White himself to take on the task of designing a suitable new home. White sketched out the plans and all the details of the new building, presenting its design to the blind Pulitzer in the form of plaster models of its parts.

The façade of the structure reflected the special needs of its owner. In contrast to the current work White and his partners were doing, the new Pulitzer house was low on surface decoration, and high on the sort of bold massing that could be readily perceived on the maquettes by the sightless fingers of Joseph Pulitzer. It looked for all the world like a Venetian palazzo on the Grand Canal *(Figure 160).* Indeed, the design was based on two seventeenth-century palaces designed for families of that city by Baldassare Longhena—the Palazzo Pesaro of 1682 and the Palazzo Rezzonico of 1667. McKim, Mead & White used the Venetian Palazzo style again in 1906 for the new building of Tiffany & Company at Fifth Avenue and East 37th Street *(Figure 161).* It is still extant, although much altered at the ground level for shops.

While the design of the outside of the house had been developed in a way that took Pulitzer's blindness into account, the interior made no such concessions. Completed in 1903, it was the sort of lavishly grand pastiche of period styles that had made Stanford White the architect and interior designer most sought out by the socially secure and the arrivistes alike *(Figures 162 & 163).* It was a visual feast that Pulitzer could hear described to him but could not enjoy himself. His nervous sensitivity to noise was, however, accommodated in the planning of his bedroom. Especially sound-resistant construction was specified, and a secondary glazed partition was erected to acoustically block the windows that overlooked the street.

These protections proved insufficient to Pulitzer's sensitive ears, and in 1904 a one-story extension was

Opposite: Figure 160. *Pulitzer's palace in 1904: the grand mansion as a private house. Although it is a multiple dwelling today, its appearance has scarcely changed. (Courtesy of The New-York Historical Society.)* Above: Figure 161. *A 1906 view of the Tiffany Building at East 37th Street and Fifth Avenue, which also looks like a Venetian palace on the Grand Canal. (Collection of Andrew Alpern.)*

built out into the end of the small side-garden of the house. This construction, designed by the specialist firm of Foster, Gade & Graham, was set as far from the street as possible, and was built with massive walls and only one small window. Ventilation was via a complex buffered duct through the roof. It was to serve as a new and silent bedroom for Pulitzer, and it connected directly with a skylit bathroom and with his study. Nonetheless, for all the cost and effort, Pulitzer still heard noises and complained that he would be driven to his death by the incessant sound.

His premonitions were possibly prophetic, for he lived in his new house for less than eight years, dying suddenly on October 29, 1911 while on board his yacht. He was buried from St. Thomas' Church following an Episcopal funeral service—a bit odd, perhaps, for one whose mother was Catholic and father was Jewish, and who was himself an agnostic. Burial was at Woodlawn Cemetery. Eschewing the grand mortuary monuments that might have been expected from one who had made his fortune by his own efforts, Joseph Pulitzer was instead buried in front of a simple Classical stone

Above, left: Figure 162. *The second-floor stair hall in Pulitzer's day, ca. 1905. The space this side of the marble columns is now part of an apartment. (Courtesy of The New-York Historical Society.)* Above, right: Figure 163. *The dark and heavy-handed dining room, which suited the tastes of the times very well, ca. 1906. It is now the living room of one of the apartments in the converted building. (Courtesy of The New-York Historical Society.)*

exedra or bench, whose only ornament is a contemplative seated bronze figure.

The grand palazzo Stanford White had designed for Joseph Pulitzer proved something of a burden. After the family had moved out, his sons were unable to find anyone who would rent it or buy it. They held it vacant for many years, finally leasing it in 1930 to a group of investors who planned on replacing the house with a new apartment structure—the fate of most of the pre–World War I mansions—but the project was abandoned. Then, in February 1934, the house was leased for 20 years to real-estate developer Henry Mandel, along with son Ralph Pulitzer's own smaller house adjoining at 17 East 73rd Street.

In the 1910s and 1920s, Mandel had been a flamboyant builder of office buildings and apartment houses, but in 1932 he declared bankruptcy, and

ultimately lost all the buildings he had constructed. In 1934, he was thinking small, and a conversion of the former Pulitzer mansion into apartments seemed appropriate.

Henry Mandel hired architect James E. Casale, and together they planned an alteration of the huge house that left untouched the majestic façade and retained the grandeur of Stanford White's interior designs. Many of the elegant high-ceilinged rooms were kept intact, with kitchens, bathrooms and hallways skillfully added to create fully functioning apartments *(Figure 164)*. Several duplexes were created and the apartment encompassing Pulitzer's "silent" bedroom and study was given its own private entrance through the garden *(Figure 165)*. The grand reception hall and staircase of the house were retained, but the huge salon—24 feet by 48 feet with a 19-foot ceiling—had to be sacrificed.

Above, left: Figure 164. *One of the elegantly detailed rooms of the former mansion, unsympathetically decorated after its conversion to the living room of Sylvia Sidney's apartment, 1954. (Gottscho-Schleisner, courtesy of the Museum of the City of New York.)* Above, right: Figure 165. *From brioche to books: The former Pulitzer breakfast room, shown in a photograph ca. 1906, is now the library of the apartment that encompasses Pulitzer's "soundproof" bedroom and study. (Courtesy of The New-York Historical Society.)*

James Casale filed plans for 17 individual apartments within the former one-family house, including one that utilized the former squash court as a double-height studio living room, and another that made use of the space formerly devoted to the basement swimming pool. Despite this, Mandel unaccountably announced in June 1934 that the lease had been returned to the Pulitzer brothers. Ralph Pulitzer's house at 17 East 73rd Street was promptly sold to Benjamin Buttenwieser, who altered it to suit his needs, and moved in the following year. The brothers themselves then did the conversion Casale had designed originally with Henry Mandel.

The apartments were rented, and in 1937 the completed venture was sold to the Astor family estate as an investment property. The estate's trustees in turn sold the building in 1952 to a construction company that planned on tearing it down and replacing it with a 12-story-and-penthouse apartment house that would incorporate the newest luxury amenity, central air-conditioning. Luckily, however, the house avoided demolition for a second time, and the Pulitzer mansion was instead converted to cooperative ownership.

Living in a multiple dwelling in New York usually means having an apartment that is exactly like many others in the same building. And so it is in other cities and in countries all over the world. But early in the nineteenth century the concept of converting a grand old mansion into distinctively unique apartments was effected, creating London's Albany. That concept was transported to New York, and the result is a mansion that retains its magnificence while still providing luxurious lodgings for a lucky 17 cooperative owners.

Toney Tenement

Co-op conversion of Vanderbilt's vision at East 77th Street and Cherokee Place

A BUILDING ON THE Upper East Side of Manhattan that offers ornate ironwork balconies, triple-hung windows that extend all the way to the floor, Piranesi-like vaulted entries, and views of the East River across a small park conjures up images of liveried elevator men and well-heeled tenants. The surprise is that the building is a six-story walk-up tenement of 1910 that was planned for families who were nursing at least one family member with tuberculosis. And doubly surprising, this tubercular tenement was designed to a level of construction and aesthetic quality unheard-of for lower-class housing, and rare even among the luxury apartment houses of its day *(Figure 166)*.

New York City in the late nineteenth century was very dramatically a city of "haves" and "have-nots." Observant people recognized that the city's poor represented a bubbling cauldron of trouble that occasionally boiled over. Essays, editorials and newspaper cartoons of the time expressed a fear that, if left unchecked, the bubbling mess might explode suddenly, as had happened several times during the 1890s in Europe, to the significant detriment of the "haves."

Much of the problem stemmed from the abysmal living conditions of the existing tenements and the attendant physical ills those crowded and unsanitary environments spawned.

Recognizing this, many of the "haves" of New York looked for ways to defuse the situation. One especially beneficial result was the tenement-house law of 1901. This reform legislation effectively stopped further construction of the infamous 25-foot "dumbbell" tenement buildings that had proved so socially disastrous. The law's restrictions and stipulations called for better light and air, improved fire safety, and private sanitary facilities for all apartments. All subsequent construction had to conform to the new law, and a number of large developments of "model" tenements was the result.

Those who were rich often had a strong vested interest in having the working class remain productive by not rioting and by not getting sick. Self-interested philanthropy was an attractive occupation for them.

The ravages of tuberculosis presented an obvious opportunity for beneficent works that would help both the laboring and the capitalist classes. For 17 years, Dr. Henry L. Shively was in charge of the tuberculosis clinic at the Presbyterian Hospital. He correctly observed that poor living conditions exacerbated the disease among the lower classes, and he sought a solution. He convinced Mrs. William K. Vanderbilt, Sr., to expend $1.5 million to endow a foundation that would construct appropriate housing for families having one or more tubercular members. (This Mrs. Vanderbilt was the *second* wife of Commodore Vanderbilt's grandson, and was *not* the mother of the unfortunate Consuelo, Duchess of Marlborough; nor was she the militant suffragette.)

Suitable property at East 78th Street and Cherokee Place was purchased, and the prominent and socially concerned architect Henry Atterbury Smith was retained to design the buildings. Dr. Shively's principles of sanitary living formed architect Smith's brief. Light and fresh air were to be maximized for each apartment, and every place where contagion might fester was to be identified and eliminated.

Drawing on the experience of a similar experiment

Figure 166. *The Cherokee cooperative apartments as they appeared in 1912, when Beaux-Arts balconies and crowning cornices were not reserved for the rich. (Courtesy of Avery Architectural Library, Columbia University.)*

in Stockholm, Sweden in 1904, and on the socially significant *Durchhäuser* of Germany and Austria, Henry Atterbury Smith created a complex of four interconnected six-story buildings. Each was centered on a large interior entrance courtyard, at whose four corners were open and balconied staircases. Protected at each level by a wire-glass canopy, these access stairs to the individual apartments were fireproof and had glazed-brick walls for easy cleaning. They were designed for easy stair-climbing, and small iron seats for resting were provided at each intermediate landing *(Figure 167).*

The individual apartments—386 of them, of two to five rooms in size—were quite exceptional for any working-class tenement, before or since. Each unit had a little entrance vestibule with a full and private bathroom adjoining. All the plumbing fittings we take for granted now as being essential for normal decent living were installed, along with electricity within each apartment—a remarkable "first" that even the much-touted City and Suburban Homes complex nearby did not provide. There were no "railroad" rooms, giving complete privacy to each bedroom.

An impervious monolithic flooring was installed throughout each apartment, with an integral six-inch-high cove baseboard that blocked vermin or accumula-

tions of dirt. Central heating was provided, with radiators mounted on the walls to prevent dirt from being hidden beneath them.

There were gas cooking stoves that had forced-air ventilating hoods above them, white porcelain sinks and glazed-wood storage cabinets. These, however, were in the combination living-dining-cooking rooms that formed the central spaces of the apartments. Generally no larger than ten by 13 feet, these "living rooms" were said to be "of moderate size to encourage simplicity in living and easy house-keeping." The bedrooms were even more "moderate" in size, the smallest being only 6' 8" wide, and the largest only a few inches wider.

Despite these limitations, the individual housing units planned by Dr. Shively, designed by Mr. Smith and financed by Mrs. Vanderbilt were a significant improvement over what had previously been available to their occupants. They offered airy, clean and decent living accommodations, as well as the opportunity for a tuberculosis sufferer to remain with his family and to receive both treatment and the training that might prevent other members of his family from contracting the debilitating disease. Balconies were provided to permit tubercular residents to spend as much time outdoors as possible, including the open-air sleeping

Above, left: Figure 167. *Piranesi for the poor: elegant access stairs, outdoors yet protected from wind and rain. Note the extra handrail placed at child-height. Photograph taken in 1912. (Courtesy of Avery Architectural Library, Columbia University.)* Above, right: Figure 168. *Tubercular terrace: balcony "bedrooms" for the consumptive surmounted by graceful cornice brackets. Photograph taken in 1912. (Courtesy of Avery Architectural Library, Columbia University.)*

that aided recovery from tuberculosis *(Figure 168)*.

Augmenting the private quarters were individual storage lockers for each family in the basement, a minihospital on the premises and a recreational roof deck that even provided toilet facilities, almost in anticipation of the rooftop health clubs atop some of the apartment houses of today *(Figure 169)*.

Known variously as the Shively Sanitary Tenements, the Vanderbilt Tenements and the East River Houses, the four-building complex remained under the ownership and management of Mrs. Vanderbilt's foundation from the time of its completion in 1912 until 1923, when the charitable trust was dissolved. The Presbyterian Hospital ran the complex temporarily, and in 1924 it was sold to the City and Suburban Homes Company, owner of an entire block of so-called model tenements across the street.

In 1985, the New York City Landmarks Preservation Commission designated the buildings as an official landmark, citing their socially important role in the battle against tuberculosis, as well as their architectural distinction. Also noted in the designation report was the prominence of the project's architect, its benefactor and its eponymous founder.

Since World War II the Shively Tenement complex has changed ownership several times. In 1986 it was renamed the Cherokee and was converted to cooperative ownership status.

In their current state, the co-oped apartments are rather different from their original form. During the 1930s, major changes were made to the units. Each apartment's kitchen functions were removed from the living room and relocated to what had been bedroom space and, wherever feasible, bedroom sizes were enlarged by reducing the total number of bedrooms on each floor. In most cases today, the then-new kitchen fittings of the 1930s have been replaced, and the original bathrooms have also been reconstructed.

During the alteration work of the 1930s, the rooftop pergolas and recreational facilities were removed. Several plans for their replacement were prepared by resident architect Terrance R. Williams,

FAIA, but none were implemented. In recognition of changed neighborhood conditions and the necessity of exercising control over access to the interior courtyards and the open stair towers, Mr. Williams also prepared designs for decorative iron security gates to block unauthorized passage through the tunnel-vaulted entrance passageways. These historically sensitive and aesthetically appropriate gateway additions have been installed.

A much more ambitious plan of Terrance Williams that was rejected as politically unworkable would have seen the demolition of the public school fronting on York Avenue to the west of the Cherokee. In its place would have been a mixed-use structure having a new school facility on the lower floors (with its own entrance) and a high-rise co-op apartment tower above that would share a new entrance court with the existing low-rise Cherokee buildings. City officials tabled the proposal, however, apparently feeling that their connection with the construction of luxury cooperative apartments somehow would be "inappropriate." As a result, the local school children must still use the antiquated nineteenth-century facilities.

The four six-story apartment buildings to the east, however, are enjoying their rejuvenation as cooperative residences. The Shively Sanitary Tenement project was constructed as an example of "enlightened philanthropy" that gave immediate benefit to its lower-class tubercular residents and their families. It also served to assuage the nervous perceptions of its upper-class patrons that the problems of the assumed-to-be-radical poor would have to be ameliorated if the existing ruling order was to be maintained. Those problems were in fact relieved. While the then-existing ruling order has been radically altered, some of its current contingent are finding it expedient to purchase apartments within these buildings that once housed an entirely different segment of the population.

It is ironic that housing once meant solely for the poor is now sought out for its distinctive architectural planning and embellishments, and that apartments once renting for a few dollars a week now command prices that exclude all but those in the upper brackets of the Internal Revenue Service's categories.

What goes in one direction surely can go in the other as well. Could it not be easily imagined that the bleak, uninspired and poorly constructed white-brick apartment houses of the 1960s scattered around the city might someday deteriorate into slum housing for the poor? If the grandly designed and solidly constructed apartment houses of the early twentieth century's expansion into the South Bronx have so quickly crumbled into dust, who is to say that the white-brick behemoths will not follow? Conversely, who is to say which elegantly designed tenement-house grouping on an obscure side street will next be rescued, restored and given new life through co-op conversion? Is it not the vitality of New York that makes changes in both these directions possible?

Figure 169. *Recreational rooftop: pleasure pavilions and the original glazed staircase skylights. Photograph taken in 1912. (Courtesy of Avery Architectural Library, Columbia University.)*

Residential Recycling

Offices to apartments in lower Manhattan

ORIGINALLY, LOWER MANHATTAN WAS all there was to New York. The entire city was clustered first around the protection of the fort at the southern tip of the island, with only outlying farms in the northern precincts. Gradually, however, the growth of the city pushed its boundaries out and up: out into the East River and the Upper Bay on newly created fill land; and up to the existing land to the north.

In classic urban-growth patterns, the expansion of commercial-space needs spread outward, pushing the residential enclaves ahead of it. Mercantile interests took over existing dwellings and converted their rooms to accommodate the functional changes of the structures. Eventually, the inadequate houses were taken down, their replacements being better suited for use as offices, manufacturing lofts and warehouses. Today, there are precious few of the original residential buildings remaining in lower Manhattan.

The small successors to the first-growth domestic architecture of Manhattan were replaced with larger buildings, and those in turn were succeeded in the late nineteenth and early twentieth centuries with office towers seen then as the pinnacle of success for the affluent businessmen of their time.

Among these were the 11-story Potter Building at Park Row and Beekman Street, and the 33-story Liberty Tower at Liberty and Nassau Streets.

The former was erected in 1883 by one-time congressman Orlando B. Potter as an investment. He maintained his own offices on the structure's top floor, and rented space in the building to those who wanted to be close to the city's governmental offices and in the heart of the newspaper and publishing section. In-cluded among the tenants were the *Press,* a penny-an-issue Republican newspaper, and the *New-York Observer,* claimed to be the city's oldest religious paper.

Designed by architect Norris G. Starkweather, who began his career in Baltimore and ended it with this building (he died in 1885), the Potter Building is distinctively and eclectically ornamental. Its façade is an intricate composition of Classical architectural interpretations, with a strong vertical emphasis. It was perhaps the first building in the city to use terra-cotta extensively as a relatively inexpensive alternative to the more traditional carved-stoned decoration. This pressed-clay material was colored to match the brick of the exterior walls, creating a coherently ornate appearance.

Terra-cotta was also employed by architect Stark-weather and builder Potter in a less visible but perhaps more important way. Specially shaped blocks of hollow terra-cotta were used here for the first time to surround the building's steel-and-iron structural framework and protect it from the heat of a fire. Structural steel had at first been thought to be inherently fireproof, since it would not burn, but it was quickly discovered that intense heat could make it buckle. With the memory of the horrendous fire in the old New York World Building on the site fresh in their minds, Starkweather and Potter were taking no chances.

The Potter Building was substantially constructed and visually pleasing and enjoyed a successful run as an office building *(Figure 170).* Later, with commercial tenants requiring larger spaces unencumbered by the

Above, left: Figure 170. *The Potter Building, ca. 1898. Light-colored awnings at some of the windows provide a primitive form of air-conditioning. Nearby are the domed tower of Joseph Pulitzer's World Building and a corner of the old Second Empire-style Post Office, both since razed. (George P. Hall, courtesy of The New-York Historical Society.)* Above, right: Figure 171. *An artist's rendering of the Liberty Tower when it was a new office building. (Courtesy of the Museum of the City of New York.)*

intrusive courtyard of pre–air-conditioning days, the structure was taken over by Pace University for its own educational needs. Eventually finding it functionally obsolescent, Pace sold the building in 1980 to Martin J. Raynes, who converted its still-sound structural envelope into a cooperative apartment house with 41 individual units.

The upper floors of the building divided themselves naturally into three sections and, with the 10-to-13-foot ceiling heights, huge spaces were a primary distinction of the units. They ranged in size from 900 to 1800 square feet apiece, and were offered as open lofts with fully equipped bathrooms and kitchens, finished floors and ceilings, but no subdividing walls. Original purchase prices were about $70 per foot, with carrying charges running $500 to $1400 per month.

The conversion of the Potter Building to residential use was part of the return of domestic occupancy to lower Manhattan that began in earnest in the mid-1970s and has continued unabated ever since.

Unusually active in this recycling work has been architect Joseph Pell Lombardi. Lombardi specialized early in the tricky area of conversions, almost exclusively taking outdated commercial structures and transforming them into apartment houses through restoration and renovation.

In 1979, he converted to residential use the office building erected in 1910 as the Liberty Tower. Built on the site of the one-time office of William Cullen Bryant's *New York Evening Post,* Liberty Tower was designed by architect Henry Ives Cobb *(Figure 171).* Presaging Cass Gilbert's Woolworth Building of 1913, Cobb developed a Gothic Revival skyscraper sheathed in cream-colored glazed terra-cotta masonry units. Unhampered by the as-yet-unwritten 1916 zoning law, Cobb created a sheer tower 33 stories high rising without a setback on a footprint only 60 by 80 feet.

Liberty Tower is composed in the manner of a Classical column—base, shaft and capital—but utilizing the verticality and ornamental detailing characteristic of the English Gothic style, albeit rather freely interpreted. The decorative treatment at the Liberty Street entrance establishes the design theme and extends upward to the fourth floor. Flanked by crocketed and pinnacled spires and surmounted by a glazed Tudor arch, the entry doors give onto a Gothic vaulted lobby finished in a marble complementary to the exterior terra-cotta. The upstairs corridors carry through the marble as wainscoting, with bronze trim.

Located in the heart of the financial district and elegantly designed and detailed, Liberty Tower was home to a distinguished tenantry, including the first New York offices of the Philadelphia accounting firm of Lybrand, Ross Brothers & Montgomery (now Coopers & Lybrand).

As with the older Potter Building, however, changing office requirements made it functionally obsolete. Few firms could use the relatively small floor sizes of about 5000 square feet apiece, and the electrical and mechanical systems were not compatible with the modern office usage of computers and other electrical equipment.

The decline of Liberty Tower's usefulness as an office building coincided with the growth of residences in lower Manhattan. Its adjacency to the landmark Chamber of Commerce building certainly contributed to its rebirth, as did its sound structural frame and skin, its unusual architectural style and a size significantly larger than would be permitted on the site by the present zoning regulations. It was a structure crying out for recycling. In 1970, there were only 1500 residential units south of Canal Street, excluding Chinatown and the Lower East Side. Ten years later that number had increased to 8000 and this redomestication has continued apace. Converting Liberty Tower into apartments was an obvious course of action.

Architect Lombardi renovated and restored the shell of the building and replaced or upgraded its electrical and mechanical systems. He brought electrical and plumbing services to each of the individual units, but left those spaces completely raw to permit purchasers to create the sorts of dwellings they might each find most individually appropriate.

Each floor was divided differently, with triplexes, duplexes and simplexes all on one level being distributed almost at random throughout the building. At the top, encompassing the space beneath the steeply pitched roofs and dormered windows, four spectacular triplex apartments were created.

Original prices for the raw units ranged from $57,000 for a 720-square-foot flat on the twenty-fourth floor (with a maintenance of $507 per month) to $225,000 for the entire twenty-ninth floor (monthly maintenance at $2002). The four garret triplexes carried prices from $179,000 to $225,000.

Architect Lombardi thought enough of the project to make a part of it his permanent home. He took space that had formerly been the boardroom and dining room of the Sinclair Oil Company and created an apartment, making the wood-paneled boardroom into his own living room. He then created the other necessary spaces using wood moldings and cabinetwork in keeping with what was retained of the remaining installations. After building a circular foyer to knit the apartment together, he furnished it with objects that might have been found in a New York home of 1910, the year Liberty Tower opened. The finishing touch was old prints on the dining-room walls depicting some of the grand ocean liners that might at one time have been seen from the windows of the now residentially recycled Liberty Tower.

Phantom Fashion

A grand cooperative apartment house at
960 Park Avenue . . . that never existed

IN THE BEGINNING, Park Avenue was considered to be on the "wrong side of the tracks"—partly because it *was* the tracks. As early as 1834, "rapid" transit cars ran on Fourth Avenue's surface-laid tracks as far north as the village of Yorkville. Three years later, a tunnel was dug through Prospect Hill from East 92nd to 94th Streets, and the railroad was able to continue further north.

Service continued to increase, prompting Commodore Vanderbilt to construct the first Grand Central Depot in 1871. Between 1872 and 1875, the tracks were lowered to a new below-grade bed, and bridges constructed at intervals to permit crosstown traffic at street level. This prompted the first hesitant residential construction along the avenue. Although confined primarily to tenement houses, it included a few hardy brownstones, as well—generally with their entrances on the side streets and their long sides to the avenue.

The sunken tracks, partially covered north of East 57th Street, were an improvement over what had been there before, and the land along Fourth Avenue between East 57th and 96th Streets was developed more and more quickly. To enhance its desirability, the street was renamed "Park Avenue" in 1888.

The new name evidently had its effect, notwithstanding the continuing smoke and fumes coming from the ventilation openings within the avenue's center malls. By the turn of the century, the street was lined with row houses, modest apartment buildings and even an occasional large mansion. It was not until 1903, however, that the state legislature decided that the smoke-belching steam locomotives would have to be replaced with ones powered by electricity.

That decision signaled a new era for Park Avenue. Only a few months after the mandate for electrification, Senator Elihu Root began constructing his new home, an elegant brick-and-limestone mansion at East 71st Street that lasted as a private house until its demolition in 1969. In anticipation of the improvement in air quality promised by the removal of smoke from the tracks, the first large luxury apartment house was erected in 1905 at East 83rd Street, according to historian Christopher Gray. The Hanover, at 983 Park Avenue, was nine stories high and had been designed by architects Neville and Bagge in a manner less than ideal. It had eight- and nine-room apartments, but they were luxurious only when compared with the small flats they replaced. They certainly would not do for anyone accustomed to living in a large and gracious town house.

In 1907, the electricity was running. At the same time, 925 Park Avenue was erected—reported by Mr. Gray to be the oldest extant apartment house on the avenue. It was designed as a cooperative by the socially prominent firm of Delano & Aldrich and consisted primarily of well-planned ten-room duplex suites, with a curious little four-room unit tucked into the rear wing of each floor. At 14 stories, and with elegant Classical detailing, 925 was the advance guard of the lavish apartment buildings that line Park Avenue today.

Into this economic environment stepped the Dudley Construction Company. It acquired control of eight buildings fronting on East 82nd Street and on Park Avenue. This gave it the entire western blockfront on the avenue from East 82nd to 83rd Street, diagonally

178

Figure 172. *The grand Italian Renaissance palazzo designed by Howells & Stokes but never built. (Collection of Andrew Alpern.)*

Figure 173. *The unbuilt design for 956 Fifth Avenue, by I. N. Phelps Stokes. (Collection of Andrew Alpern.)*

across from the Hanover, and two blocks north of 925 Park.

The company engaged the architectural firm of Howells & Stokes to design a grand apartment house. A more impressive firm would have been hard to find. While John Mead Howells was skilled and socially well connected, his partner, Isaac Newton Phelps Stokes, was even more prosperous and well known. Stokes was an advocate of improved housing for the working classes (in 1900, he had been appointed by President Theodore Roosevelt to a commission on tenement houses) and he would later produce the massive six-volume compendium *The Iconography of Manhattan Island.*

The design produced by Howells & Stokes was grandly impressive. A 12-story approximation of an Italian Renaissance palace, the building was massive, but this was moderated by careful design and architectural detail. The three street façades were each divided horizontally into three main sections with full-story belt-course separations and a corresponding belt course just below the huge projecting cornice. There were to be arched windows, colonnettes, balconies, balustrades, paneled spandrels, cartouches, a rusticated base section and three grandly arched entrances *(Figure 172).*

Inside, there were to be 54 apartments, all large and functionally arranged with spacious rooms and short circulation hallways that emanated from large central foyers. Multiple amenities were also planned for gracious living and large-scale entertaining. Six of the apartments—three duplexes and three triplexes—were to have private street entrances. Fifteen duplex suites and 33 simplex flats would be upstairs, ranging in size from nine to 13 rooms. The features were to include additional storage rooms in the basement (within the building and under the sidewalk).

The offering prices ranged from $24,000 to $52,000, with average maintenance costs running from $245 to $420 per month. It was proposed that the cooperative corporation would own half the apartments, with the income from the market-rate rentals of those units used to reduce the effective cost of the apartments occupied by the stockholders of the corporation.

The prospectus for this grand project was dated June 1910 and anticipated the completion of the building by September 1, 1912. The developer had an out, however, by stipulating that all contracts for the sale of individual apartments could be canceled during the first two weeks of April 1911, if by that time it had not secured final and good title to the property, or if it were not able to obtain a building loan for $1.2 million.

All should have gone well if the publicity brochure is to be believed:

> [The site] adjoins the best residential section of Fifth and Madison avenues, and is in the heart of the finest private residence development on Park Avenue, the permanent character of which, both above and below this point, is now assured. It enjoys all the advantages of close proximity to Central Park—two blocks to the west. The unusual width of Park Avenue insures an abundance of air and sunshine. The Lexington Avenue Subway (one block to the east), the immediate construction of which has been authorized, will shortly add to the present accessibility of the location and make it an unusually convenient residential section.

The building, too, was highly touted:

> The building itself will be of the best fireproof construction throughout, substantially built, especial consideration being given to the sound-proof qualities of the walls and floors. The exterior will be of Norman brick with stone trim, of simple and dignified design, free from excessive and unnecessary ornamentation. There will be three main entrances, each leading to a separate elevator, which in turn gives access to not more than two apartments on each floor landing. The effect of this arrangement will be to bring the individual apartment entrances as directly as possible into contact with the street, and make each resemble, as closely as may be, the outer entrance to a private dwelling, giving a sense of individuality and privacy not elsewhere attained in American apartment houses.

Reference was also made to the service and secondary elements of the venture:

> Upon a portion of the roof will be arranged a promenade with shelters and seats, and also a playground for children. These will be suitably separated from the laundry and drying rooms, which will occupy another section of the roof.
>
> In the apartments themselves, unusual attention has been given to the niceties of planning and design in even the smallest details, with especial reference to the maintenance of correct proportions throughout: the concealment of all disfiguring columns, girders and pipes; the proper location of fireplaces; the centering of windows; etc., etc. There will be noted—An absence of long corridors. The large size and excellent proportion of the rooms. Ceilings are over ten feet high in the clear. A vacuum cleaning plant will be installed, with an outlet in each apartment. The principal rooms in each apartment will be provided with open fireplaces for coal or wood fires. Entrance halls with high wainscoting. Dining Rooms and Libraries in old English Oak. Bathrooms in marble, tile, and white enamel.

All this came to naught, however. The 960 Park Avenue designed by Howells & Stokes was never built. The reasons are probably buried in papers long since destroyed. But a clue may exist in the level of design detail called for by architect I. N. Phelps Stokes. Stokes was used to having the best in his personal life and may have been incapable of the compromises necessary to any large construction venture. This theory is supported by what happened in 1923: Stokes designed a seven-unit apartment house at 956 Fifth Avenue on the south corner of East 77th Street that also died on the drawing board. That project was planned as an enlarged interpretation of a domestic building of the Italian Renaissance, with apartment units that Stokes himself would doubtless have felt comfortable living in. Gracious architecture, but impractical economics (*Figure 173*).

Ultimately, a different, perhaps more pragmatic, architect designed the 956 Fifth Avenue that exists today. And ultimately a different 960 Park Avenue was constructed as well.

Architectural design is a combination of engineering and art. It must function well and it must look appropriate and attractive. But in the end, the architect must understand the needs of the marketplace, and must design a structure with a cost that can be justified by the potential cash flow and profit. No matter how well planned or elegantly detailed, a building that is not designed with the economic realities of its time and place in mind will end as the original 960 Park Avenue did—a paper phantom, beautiful to behold, but impossible to build.

Shrinking Space

The evolving New York–apartment floor plan

SPACE: THE LAST FRONTIER. It might be the catchy title for a book about a trip to Mars or a voyage through the Milky Way. But it also addresses a perennial problem of apartment dwellers: Sufficient space is never affordably available. Layouts are either cramped and mean or astronomically expensive. Conventional wisdom asserts that things were better in the old days, but the rose-colored glass that is nostalgia is selective in its vision, and consequently distorts reality.

The earliest units, constructed in the 1870s, were not particularly spacious. While most had living rooms, dining rooms and multiple bedrooms, almost all had no more than a single bathroom. They also had primitive planning: circulation patterns were circuitous and awkwardly placed doors and windows hampered furniture placement. The concepts of spatial sequences just did not exist.

The architects and builders worried more about high ceilings and decorative moldings than functional planning. The moldings, though a cherished feature, were often thoughtlessly placed. If the opening was too close to a wall, the door frame was inappropriately cut off. Decorations were usually added as an afterthought and were seldom used to determine the position of other architectural elements. The high ceilings helped keep apartments cool in the summers before air-conditioning, but in winter the rising heat made such spaces cold and uncomfortable. A further disadvantage was the uniform ceiling heights: What was proportional in a living room was no longer so in a small bedroom or corridor. Perhaps apartment shoppers of the era back then did not know any better, but what they got for their money was far from perfect.

Beginning in the 1880s and continuing for about 45 years, apartment planning improved significantly. A broad range of well-designed unit layouts was available to suit almost any budget. Social customs had a strong influence on the change. At the beginning of the twentieth century many one-bedroom apartments included a dining room, and sometimes even a small servant's bedroom. *Upstairs Downstairs* merely became horizontal in the New York apartment. But not until the century was well under way did multiple bathrooms become the norm. Indeed, the lack of full bathroom facilities for servants did not completely disappear until that time. And it was only the decline in the taste for Victorian wardrobe furniture that brought about a demand for the sort of closets we now take for granted.

Prior to World War I, large "family" apartments with four or more bedrooms were not at all uncommon. Nine- and ten-room apartments were the staple of the luxury trade. Some units had up to 18 rooms (such as 903 Park Avenue; *Figure 174*), yet most were of the "long hall" variety since development sites were too constrained to permit gracious room arrangements. There were exceptions, but these were produced mostly by architectural firms such as Schwartz & Gross, which specialized almost exclusively in apartment-house planning and design. Most other architects evidently did not have the skill to produce good layouts.

From the Armistice to the stock-market crash of 1929, apartment-house planning developed into a high art. Extensive use was made of the entrance foyer or gallery, which opened onto the dining room, the living room and a foreshortened hallway that led to

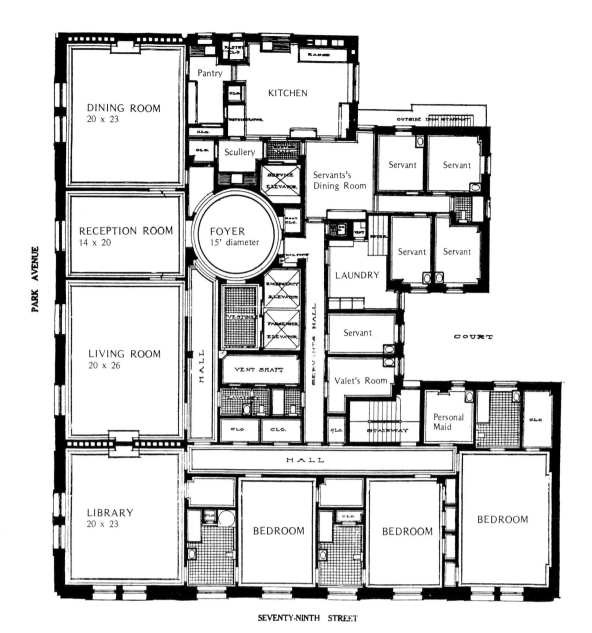

Above: Figure 174. *An 18-room full-floor apartment at 903 Park Avenue that would have served as a substitute for a large town house. (Collection of Andrew Alpern.)* Below: Figure 175. *A one-bedroom apartment in the Century Apartments at 25 Central Park West that can fit entirely within the space of the dining room and small reception room of the apartment at 903 Park Avenue, shown in Figure 174. (Collection of Andrew Alpern.)*

the bedrooms. The most rarified of these plans were produced by Rosario Candela and by J. E. R. Carpenter, whose grand buildings now represent the finest living accommodations in New York. Following closely was Emery Roth, the immigrant architect who founded the firm that now bears his name. The ubiquitous Schwartz & Gross also produced off-the-foyer plans for countless Manhattan apartment houses of the teens and twenties.

A large number of very grand and gracious "studio" apartments were created during the period from around 1900 to World War I, and a large percentage still exist. The greatest concentration is on West 67th Street, where the glories of the huge two-storied living rooms are hidden behind unassuming façades. Similarly spacious apartments with double-height spaces

still stand on Central Park South (the Gainsborough Studios), at Lexington Avenue and East 66th Street (the limestone masterpiece of Charles A. Platt) and at the spectacular (if somewhat later) 322 East 57th Street.

During the 1920s, the special apartments were usually more "conventional" duplexes. Certain buildings contained only such apartments, which seemed like spacious private houses. Most had a level of quality and detail not seen today, albeit obtainable then only at a very high price. More than mere snob appeal has concentrated so many multimillion dollar apartments—the suites *are* palpably better at 834 Fifth Avenue, 960 Fifth Avenue and 740 Park Avenue.

Most of the city's spectacularly large apartments were created in that period. A palatial habitat was built for Arthur Brisbane in the Ritz Tower at Park Avenue and East 57th Street, followed almost immediately by a second (also for Brisbane) of equally grand proportions at 1215 Fifth Avenue. (This has been subdivided, but the one on Park Avenue is still intact and privately occupied.)

At the same time, Macy's head Jesse Isidor Straus occupied a huge two-floor apartment at 720 Park Avenue. His home included a 40-foot entrance gallery, a 36-foot library, separate wine and vegetable closet, a valeting room, a sewing room and a kitchen larger than most modern living rooms.

The grandest of all was the 54-room triplex of Mr. and Mrs. E. F. Hutton at 1107 Fifth Avenue. The size of that apartment was appropriate to the grand scale of the couple's parties.

The Great Depression put a damper on the lifestyles that justified lavish apartments. Even ordinary units proved too expensive for most. Many of the large apartments were subdivided into more marketable dwellings, and those constructed during the 1930s were far smaller than their predecessors *(Figure 175)*.

World War II, however, stopped all apartment-house construction dead in its tracks. When building resumed in the 1950s and 1960s, it appeared that something besides people had died in the war. The designs were bleak, mean, ungracious, cramped and thoughtless. The ubiquitous white glazed brick, cheap aluminum windows, low ceilings, boxlike rooms and nonexistent foyers, hallways and dining rooms, made for a cookie-cutter sort of architecture. You had to look at the street signs to tell where you were, and at the size of the monthly payments to convince yourself that you were not in some municipal housing project for the needy.

During the 1980s two seemingly conflicting trends emerged. On the one side, rising land and construction costs have forced builders to shrink dimensions. Entire one-bedroom apartments are now smaller than what was formerly a decent-size living room. Two-bedroom units are carved out of space once considered minimal for a bachelor pad. And three- or four-bedroom apartments are almost obsolete.

On the other hand, imaginative (or profit-oriented) developers are creating distinctively different layouts. In the late 1970s, 800 Fifth Avenue was considered daring because the entrance galleries had curved walls. Later, conversion of nonresidential buildings into apartment houses gave opportunities for oddly shaped rooms, and interior balconies could fit into the high-ceilinged spaces. More recently, a building that uses curved walls as an essential design theme has gone up overlooking the entrance to the Queens Midtown Tunnel. The curves are in the exterior window walls, as well as in the rounded corners of the "galleries." The technique, however, is a gimmick that obscures, but not entirely, the contorted planning. The building was created around a marketing concept, rather than as a natural outgrowth of the internal needs of its apartments.

Apartment sizes are not what they used to be; the space has shrunk. The "extra" space is missing. Gone are the entrance foyers that were really separate rooms without windows, hallways wide enough for bookcases down one side, circulation patterns that allowed for "mingling" at a party, and of course, the study, library, extra bedroom or "spare" room.

The reasons are purely economic . . . or are they? True enough, union builders now earn vastly more in real terms than workers of the 1920s. True enough, the other costs—hard and soft—that affect the dwelling price have gone up disproportionately to the general cost of living. But is that the only reason why dining rooms, servants' quarters and wide hallways are no longer common?

It is a question of life-style. In this age of computers and video-tape players, are long walls capable of housing vast libraries still needed? With restaurants on almost every street, and late working hours the order of the day, is there really a place for a formal dining room? And with the little retreat at the beach or up in the mountains, and far-flung vacations accessible even to the novice computer operator, is there justification for extra rooms?

Life in Gotham is a continuum of change. But are our living patterns changing too fast? Shorn of all theory, we are indeed surrounded by shrinking space. The good old days may not really have been as good as our nostalgic memories would have us believe, but at least you could move around in them.

Index

Akron Building Company, 88
Albany (London), 12–16, 165, 169
Albany Apartments, 3
Alger, Horatio, 135
Allaire, James, 38
Alwyn Court Apartments, 52, 94–97, 108
Ambassador Hotel, 105
American Fine Arts Society, 27
American Institute of Architects, 24, 135
American Institute of Architects' Gold
    Medal Award (1916), 109
American Museum of Natural History, 52,
    67, 73, 136
American Weekly, 119
Anderson, Mrs. Millbank, 117, 119
Anderson, Mrs. Millbank, residence, 117, 119
Andrews, Roy Chapman, 49
Angell, Edward, 67, 68
Ansonia Hotel, 33–37
Antony and Cleopatra, 157
Apthorp Apartments, 58, 59
Architectural League, 27
Architectural Record, The, 54
Arizona Apartments, 4
Armstrong, Edwin, 153
Arnoux, Judge William H., 24
Arts & Decoration, 122
Art Students League, 27
Art Students League building, 27, 30
Astor, John Jacob, 38, 39, 161
Astor, William Waldorf, 59, 61, 88
Astor family estate, 169
Astor House, 38, 39, 161
Atlantic Terra Cotta Company, 143

Ball, Alwyn, Jr., 94
Banner, Peter, 69, 70, 71
Barberini Palace, 120
Barcelona Apartments, 3, 21
Barney, Charles Tracy, 167
Barstun Realty Company, 71
Baruch, Bernard, 109
Beach, Alfred Ely, 77
Beau Séjour Apartments, 3
Beck, Martin, 119
Beebe, William, 49
Beecham, Sir Thomas, 15
Belgrave Square (London), 63
Bell, Byron, 48
Belmont, August, 77
Belnord Apartments, 22, 61
Belnord Realty Company, 61
Belvedere Castle, 72
Beresford Apartments, 135–139
Berkeley Apartments, 3
Berkshire Apartments, 3
Bernhardt, Sarah, 161
Bethesda Terrace and Fountain, 72
Beyer Blinder Belle, 97
Bing, Alexander, 105
Bing, Leo, 105
Bing & Bing, 93, 105, 135

Bitter, Karl, 52
Blenheim Apartments, 3
BMT (Brooklyn–Manhattan Transit) sub-
    way, 111
Booth, Edwin, 66
Bordeaux Apartments, 3
Bottomley, William L., 151
Bottomley, William L., apartment, 152, 153
Bottomley, Wagner & White, 151
Bowen, E. Cochrane, 132
Bowery Savings Bank, 125
Brentmore Apartments, 41, 42
Bricken Construction Company, 61, 110
Brisbane, Arthur, 122, 182
Broadway subway line, *see* IRT
Broun, Heywood, 49
Brown, David, 137
Brown, Helen Gurley, 137
Bryant, William Cullen, 176
Buckham, Charles W., 40
Buckingham Palace Apartments, 3
Buckley, William F., Jr., 41
Burden, I. T., house (former), 113
Burden, James A., Jr., 153
Burden family, 153
Burke, Billie, 35
Burlington House (London), 15
Burnham's Tavern, 59
Butler, Eddie, 89
Buttenwieser, Benjamin, 169
Byron, Lord, 15

Cadogan Gardens (London), 63
Café des Artistes, 43, 48
Campagna, Anthony, 109
Campbell, James, 24
Candela, Rosario, 105, 109, 181
Capital Cities/ABC television center, 43
Carey, Hugh, 49
Carlyle Apartments, 3
Carnegie Hall, 27, 90, 94
Carpenter, J. E. R., 109, 110, 181
Carrère & Hastings, 157
Caruso, Enrico, 26, 35
Casale, James E., 168, 169
Cauldwell-Wingate (builder), 105
Cayuga Apartments, 3
Central Park, 22, 27, 44, 67, 72, 74, 83, 94,
    97, 109, 111, 137, 179
Central Park Apartments (a.k.a. Navarro
    Apartments; Spanish Flats), 6, 21–23,
    27, 94
Central Park Livery Stables, 27
Central Park Menagerie, 35
Central Park South, 135
Central Park West
    No. 101, 162
Central Savings Bank building (former), 125
Century Apartments, 102, 137, 157–160, 161,
    181
Century Theatre, 157, 158
Chaliapin, Fyodor, 35

Chambellan, René, 164
Chamber of Commerce building, 176
Chanin, Irwin S., 157, 158, 160, 161, 162, 164
Chanin Construction Company, 161
Chase, William Merritt, 39
Chatsworth Apartments, 3, 77, 78, 81
Chelsea Cottages, 145
Chelsea Hotel, 17, 19, 20
Chelsea House, 145, 147, 148
Cherbourg Apartments, 3
Cherokee Apartments, *see* East River Houses
Christy, Howard Chandler, 48
Church, Frederick, 39
City and Suburban Homes, 171
City and Suburban Homes Company, 172
City College building (East 23rd Street), 66
City Hall Park, 77
Clark, Edward, 5, 6, 57, 72
Clarke, Captain and Mrs. Thomas, 145, 147,
    150
Cleva, Fausto, 35
Clinton and Russell, 59
Cloud, Agnes, Residence, 147
Cobb, Henry Ives, 176
Cole, Alphæus, 17
Columbia College, 145
Columbia University, 97
Commissioners' Street Map (1811), 63
Comstock, Anthony, 29
Consuelo, Duchess of Marlborough, 170
Cooper, Peter, 64, 66
"Cooperative Apartment House Built to
    Meet the Owners' Tastes, A," 113
Cooper-Hewitt house, 64, 66
Coopers & Lybrand, 176
Cooper Union, 66
Copland, Alexander, 12
Cordova Apartments, 3, 21
Corning, Edward, 66
Cornwall Apartments, 3
Costello, Frank, 164
Coward, Noël, 49
Cowles, Fleur, 15
Cross & Cross, 105
Cushing, Harry, 153
Cutting family, 153

Da Cunha, George W., 24
Dairy (Central Park), 72
Dakota Apartments, 5, 6, 27, 55, 57, 67, 69,
    72, 136, 161
Daly's Theatre, 157
Davis, Alexander Jackson, 64
Davis, John W., 114, 115
Delamarre, Jacques, 164
Delano & Aldrich, 130, 177
Delmonico's, 26
Department of Buildings, 2, 88, 151, 156
de Wolfe, Elsie, 130
Dickens, Charles, 15
Dilworth, Mrs. Joseph, 115
Dry Dock Savings Bank, 95, 97

Duboy, Paul Emile, 33, 35
Dudley Construction Company, 177
Duggin and Crossman, 29
Duncan, Isadora, 26, 49
Duncraggan Apartments, 3
Dundonald Apartments, 3
Dunsbro Apartments, 3
Dunwell Apartments, 3

East River Houses (a.k.a. Cherokee Apartments; Shively Sanitary Tenements; Vanderbilt Tenements), 170–173
École des Beaux-Arts, 69, 88
Edward VII, 48
Edward, Prince of Wales, 49
80th Street, East
   No. 525, 42
El Casco Apartments, 3
Eldorado Apartments, 102
El Dorado Hotel, 161
El Greco Apartments, 3
Ellinger, Edgar, 96, 97
El Nido Apartments, 3
Enid Apartments, 3
Eton Place (London), 63

Falwell, Jerry, 29
Farrar, Geraldine, 26, 35
Farrar, Victor, 148
Farrar & Watmough, 148
Feder, Abe, 48
Fellini's Satyricon, 10
Ferber, Edna, 49, 161
Field, Cyrus West, and brother, 64, 65
Field, Marshall, III, 153
Fifth Avenue
   No. 51, 40
   No. 551, 134
   No. 666, 126
   No. 810, 110–112
   No. 812, 112
   No. 817, 110, 112
   No. 820, 110, 111
   No. 825, 110, 111
   No. 834, 109–110, 156, 182
   No. 845 (a.k.a. 4 East 66th Street), 109
   No. 907, 108–109, 110
   No. 956, 178, 179
   No. 960, 182
   No. 998, 105
   No. 1010, 130–134
   No. 1040, 130, 131
   No. 1107, 113–116
   No. 1140, 130
   No. 1215, 122, 182
Fifth Avenue Coach Company, 77
55th Street, East
   No. 10, 167
57th Street, East
   No. 322, 182
Fiske, Haley, 24
Fitch, Dr. James Marston, 97
Fledgeby, Fascination, 15
Fogg Museum, 44
Forsch, Albert, 71
Foster, Gade & Graham, 167
Framley Parsonage, 15
Franklin Delano Roosevelt Drive, 154
Frederick, Duke of York and Albany, 12, 165
French, Cordelia, 132, 134
French, Ellen Millard (Mrs. Ernest McKay), 134
French, Frederick Fillmore, 130, 131, 132, 133, 134
French, Frederick Fillmore, apartment, 130–134
French, Frederick Fillmore, Jr., 134
French, John Winslow, 134
French, Theodore, 134
Friars Club building, 119
Fuchs, Emil, 46, 48

Fuller, George A., Construction Company, 113
Fulton, Robert, 80
Furness, Frank, 39
Furniss, William P., residence, 84

Gainsborough Studios, 40, 41, 182
Garrison, Lindley, 115
Garth, David, 49
Gatti-Casazza, Giulio, 35
General Theological Seminary, 145
George III, 12, 63
Gerlach, Charles, 24, 26
Gibbons, Douglas, 113
Gilbert, Cass, 176
Gladstone, William, 15
Goldberger, Paul, 49
Goldstone, Lafayette Anthony, 4, 80, 98, 124
Gould, Jay, 165
Gracie Square
   No. 10, 155
Graham Court Apartments, 57, 59
Gramercy Apartments, 17, 24–26, 27
Gramercy Family Hotel, 24
Gramercy Hotel, 66
Gramercy Park, 24, 26, 63, 64, 66
Gramercy Park House, 24
Granada Apartments, 3, 21
Grand Central Depot, 103, 177
Grand Central Terminal, 100, 101, 102, 105, 106
Gray, Christopher, 5, 17, 134, 156, 177
Green, Andrew Haswell, 83
Greene, Graham, 15
Grenoble Hotel, 3, 27
Gross, Arthur, 89
Grosvenor Apartments, 3
Guild of Masons, House of the (Ghent), 93
Gutfreund, John and Susan, 156

Haas, Richard, 97
Haines, Franklin, 74
Haines, Samuel, 74
Hamilton Apartments, 3, 86
Hanover Apartments, 177
Harde, Herbert Spencer, 52, 91, 93, 94
Harde & Short, 40, 52, 54, 55, 91, 93, 94
Hardenbergh, Henry Janeway, 5, 27, 57
Harder, Julius, 105
Hare, J. Montgomery, 115
Harmonie Club, 68
Harnick, Sheldon, 137
Hart, Tillie, 148
Hastings, Thomas, 135
Hauptmann, Bruno Richard, 164
Hearst, William Randolph, 122, 165
Hearst, William Randolph, apartment, 122, 123
Hearst organization, 119
Heath, Edward, 15
Heddon Construction Company, 94
Hendrik Hudson Apartments, 77–82
Henry VIII, 120
Hewitt, Abram, 64
Hicks, David, 15
Hirschfeld, Abe, 112
Hoffman, F. Burrall, Jr., 126
Hogan, Frank, 90
Hohen-Au Apartments, 3
Hohenzollern Apartments, 3
Holland, Henry, 12, 13, 15
Holzer, Jacob Adolphus, 29
Homer, Winslow, 39
Hotel Belleclaire, 135
Hotel Beresford (1889), 67, 135, 136, 161
Hotel des Artistes, 40, 43–51, 52, 76
Hotel Majestic, 73, 161, 162
Hotel San Remo, 67, 161, 162
Hoving, Walter, 153
Howells, John Mead, 117, 178
Howells & Stokes, 178

HRH Construction Company, 136
Hubert, Philip Gengembre, 17–23, 24, 27
Hubert Home Clubs, 17, 20, 21, 23
Hubert, Pirsson & Company, 6, 17
Hudson, Henry, 80
Hudson Fulton Celebration (1909), 80, 81
Hunt, Richard Morris, 23, 39, 40, 165
Hurok, Sol, 35
Hurst, Fannie, 44
Hutton, Mr. and Mrs. Edward F., and family, 113, 114, 153
Hutton, Mr. and Mrs. Edward F., apartment, 114–116, 182
Hutton, Mr. and Mrs. Edward F., residence, 113, 114
Huxley, Aldous, 15
Huxtable, Ada Louise, 71

Iconography of Manhattan Island, The, 178
Idaho Apartments (850 Seventh Avenue), 4
Idaho Apartments (153 East 48th Street), 4, 98
Illinois Apartments, 4
Importance of Being Earnest, The, 15
Indiana Apartments (117 West 79th Street), 4
Indiana Apartments (127 West 82nd Street), 4
IND (Independent) subway, 136
Internal Revenue Service, U.S., 55, 173
"In the Kitchen," 7
"In the Parlor," 7
Iroquois Apartments, 3
IRT (Interborough Rapid Transit) subway, 77, 86, 111
Iselin family, 153

Jacobs, Harry Allan, 117, 119, 120
Jacobs, Robert, 119
Jardine, David, 3
Jennings, Arthur B., 85
Johnson, George F., Jr., 77, 80
Johnson and Kahn, 77, 78, 80

Kafka, Hugo, 27
Kahn, Aleck, 77, 80
Kahn, Ely Jacques, 119
Kahn, Otto, 119
Kahn & Jacobs, 105, 119
Kalikow, Peter, 33
Kansas City Post, 108
Kilpatrick, General John Reed, 113
Kissinger, Henry, 153
Knickerbocker Village, 134
Kobler, A. J., 117, 119, 120, 122
Kobler, A. J., apartment, 120–122
Korn, Louis, 68
Kreisler, Fritz, 153

La Farge, John, 39
Lafayette Apartments, 3
La Guardia, Fiorello, 83
Lamb, Thomas W., 40
Lamb & Rich, 103
Landmarks Preservation Commission, 37, 71, 93, 135, 172
Langham Apartments, 69, 136
Langham Hotel, 29
Lawrence, Alexander M., 64
Lehman, Herbert, 119
Levi, Julian Clarence, 30
Lewis, Albert W., 42
Lewisohn, Adolph, 119
Lexington, Battle of, 64
Lexington Avenue
   No. 1, 63–66
   No. 9, 64
Lexington Avenue subway, 179
Ley, Fred T., Company, 110
Liberace, 9
Liberty, 165
Liberty Tower, 174, 175, 176
Lincoln Center for the Performing Arts, 127

Lindsay, John V., 49
Lisbon Apartments, 21
Loeb, Kuhn, banking firm, 115
Logan, Joshua, 153
Lombardi, Joseph Pell, 175, 176
Lombardy Apartments, 142
London Terrace (1845), 145, 147
London Terrace (1929–31), 142, 145–150
London Terrace Gardens, 150
London Terrace Towers, 150
Longhena, Baldassare, 167
Lucas, Herbert, 66
Lufton, Lord, 15
Lybrand, Ross Brothers & Montgomery, 176
Lyons, Leonard, 137
Lyons, Robert T., 69

Macaulay, Thomas Babington, 15
Mackenzie, Compton, 16
Macy's, 182
Madison Avenue
    No. 121, 17
    No. 777 (a.k.a. 45 East 66th Street), 93
Madrid Apartments, 3, 21
Mahler, Gustav, 73, 161
Majestic Apartments, 102, 137, 161–164
Majestic Theatre, 157
Mandel, Henry, 140, 142, 144, 148, 150, 168, 169
Mandel-Ehrich Corporation, 140
Manhattan Square, 52, 67, 73, 136
Marcos, Ferdinand, 129
Marcos, Imelda, 127, 129
Marcus, Mrs. Stanley, 127
Marguery Hotel, 105
Markham, Edwin, 26
Markwood, Valerie, 48
Martin, William R., 83
Masque Theatre, 157
Mayfair Apartments, 103, 105
McComb, J. Jennings, 23
McKay, Mrs. Ernest (Ellen Millard French), 134
McKim, Charles Follen, 105
McKim, Mead & White, 24, 68, 126, 167
Mead, Margaret, 137
Melba, Nellie, 26
Melbourne, Lord and Lady, 12, 13
Melbourne House (London), 15, 165
Melchior, Lauritz, 35
Memphis Uptown Apartments, 9
Merrill, Dina, 153
Metropolitan Life Insurance Company, 24
Metropolitan Opera House (1883), 73
"Millionaire's Row," 147
Mills, J. Layng, 126
Miss America Beauty Pageant, 48
Montana Apartments (Broadway), 102
Montana Apartments (155 East 48th Street), 98
Montana Apartments (375 Park Avenue), 98–102
Montana Apartments (West 124th Street), 98
Moore, Benjamin and Charity Clarke, 145
Moore, Clement Clarke, 145, 147, 148
Morgan, J. Pierpont, 30
Morris, Newbold, 89
Mott, Valentine, 3
Mount Morris Park, 98
multiple-dwelling law (1929), 120, 138, 148, 151, 162
Murray, Mae, 35

Nast, Albert E., 142
Nast, Condé, 130, 131
Naumburg, Aaron, 44, 46, 49
Naumburg Band Shell (Central Park), 44
Navarro, José (Juan) de, 21, 135
Navarro Apartments, see Central Park Apartments
Nevada Apartments, 4

Neville and Bagge, 177
New Theatre, 157
New York Architectural Terra-Cotta Company, 35
New York Athletic Club, 23
New York Cancer Hospital, 67
New York Central Railroad, 105
New York Edison Company, 26
New York Evening Post, 176
New-York Historical Society, 125
New-York Observer, 174
New York Public Library (Fifth Avenue/West 42nd Street), 157
New York State Theater, 127
New York Times, 37, 43, 49, 76, 117, 126
New York Times Sunday magazine, 125
New York World, 165
New York World Building, 174, 175
Nichols, Mike, 137
Nicholson & Galloway, 55
Niebuhr, Reinhold, 90
Nijinsky, Vaslav, 161
Ninth Avenue Elevated Railway, 72, 77
Nixon, Richard Milhous, 112, 156
Noakes, George, residence, 83, 85, 86

Ohio Apartments, 4
Olmsted, Frederick Law, 83
Onondaga Apartments, 3
Onward Construction Company, 35
Opper, Frederick Burr, 7
Oregon Apartments, 4
Osborne, Thomas, 6, 29, 30
Osborne Apartments (Fifth Avenue), 29
Osborne Apartments (205 West 57th Street), 6, 27–32, 94
Otis Brothers & Company, 26
Our Mutual Friend, 15

Pace University, 175
Palais de France, 157
Palermo Apartments, 3
Paris Apartments, 3
Park Avenue
    No. 1, 142
    No. 270, 105, 106
    No. 277, 105
    No. 290, 105
    No. 320, 105
    No. 400, 105
    No. 410, 104, 105
    No. 417, 102, 103–107
    No. 420–430, 105, 106
    No. 445, 105, 106
    No. 471, 40, 41
    No. 660, 124, 125
    No. 666, 124–129
    No. 740, 182
    No. 760, 124
    No. 820, 117–123
    No. 898, 140–144, 148
    No. 903, 180, 181
    No. 925, 177, 178
    No. 960, 177–179
    No. 1185, 61, 62
Park Hotel, see Astor House
Park Lane Hotel, 105
Parkview Apartments, 93
Pavlova, Anna, 161
Pearsall, William R., 126
Pennington, Pleasants, 42
Pershing Square Building, 140
Pesaro, Palazzo, 167
Phelps, Anson Greene, 35
Phelps/Dodge/Stokes family, 33
Phibro Corporation, 156
Phyfe, John Duncan, 24
Phyfe, William Duncan, 24
Pierpont Morgan Library, 30
Pinza, Ezio, 35

Piranesi, Giambattista, 172
Platt, Charles A., residence, 182
Plaza Hotel (1890), 24
Pollard, George Mort, 43
Pollard & Steinam, 43
Pons, Lily, 35
Poor, Henry W., 64, 65
Poor, Henry W., mansion, 64, 65
Pope, Virginia, 125, 126
Porter, Seton, 126, 127
Porter, Seton, apartment, 126–127
Post, George B., 39
Postal Life building, 140
Postel, Robert and Joan, 156
Post Office, U.S., building (former), 175
Post Toasties, 114
Potter, E. Clifford, 98
Potter, Fred G., 98
Potter, Orlando B., 174
Potter Building, 174–175, 176
Prasada Apartments, 72–76, 136
Pratt, Ruth Baker, 153
Pratt family, 153
Presbyterian Hospital, 170, 172
Press, 174
Price, Thomas, 38
Priestley, J. B., 15
Prisoner Without a Name, Cell Without a Number, 89
Progress Club, 68, 69, 71
Pulitzer, Joseph, 165, 167, 168, 175
Pulitzer, Joseph, residence, 165–169
Pulitzer, Ralph, residence, 168, 169
Pulitzer family, 168, 169
Pulitzer Fountain, 165
Pulitzer Prizes, 165

Queens Midtown Tunnel, 182

Rambusch Studios, 30, 32
Randall, Tony, 137
Ranger, Henry W., 43
Rattigan, Terence, 15
Raynes, Martin J., 175
Real Estate Record and Guide, 29, 68, 94
Red House Apartments, 52, 93
Rembrandt Apartments, 17, 18, 24, 27
Restell, Madame, 29
Rezzonico, Palazzo, 167
Rice, Isaac, mansion, 83
Rich & Mathesius, 43
Richelieu, Duc de, 26
Rio Apartments, 9
Ritz Tower, 182
River Club, 151, 153
River House, 151–156
Riverside Drive
    No. 137, 122, 123
    No. 404, 83–90
Riverside Mansions, 86
Riverside Park, 33, 67, 78, 80, 83, 89
Roberts, Mary Fanton, 122
Rochambeau Apartments, 3
Rockefeller, Margaretta Fitler ("Happy") Murphy, 112
Rockefeller, Mary Todhunter Clark, 111
Rockefeller, Nelson, 111, 112
Rockefeller Center, 22
Rockefeller family, 109, 153
Rockwell, Norman, 48
Rogers, Isaiah, 38
Roma Apartments, 3
Romberg, Sigmund, 161
Romeyn, Charles W., 74
Roosevelt, Theodore, 178
Roosevelt Island, 155
Root, Elihu, 177
Root, Elihu, residence, 177
Rose Apartments, 3
Roth, Emery, 105, 106, 135, 136, 138, 181
Rothzeid, Bernard, 42

Rouse, William Lawrence, 78, 80, 81, 82, 98, 113, 124
Rouse and Goldstone, 80, 98, 113, 124
Rouse and Sloan, 78, 98
Royale Theatre, 157
Royal Hospital (Chelsea, London), 145
Rudd, Carrington, mansion, 83, 85, 86
Ruggles, Samuel Bulkley, 63, 64
Russell, Walter, 43, 51, 52, 76
Russian Tea Room, 17
Ruttenbaum, Steven, 136

Sackler, Dr. Arthur, 129
Saint Catherine Apartments, 27
St. John the Divine, Cathedral Church of, 77
St. Louis Dispatch, 165
St. Louis Post, 165
St. Louis Post-Dispatch, 165
St. Paul's Chapel, 161
St. Paul's Chapel (Trinity Parish), 38
St. Peter's Episcopal Church, 145
St. Thomas' Church, 167
St. Urban Apartments, 67–71
Salamanca Apartments, 3
Salomon Brothers, 156
Salwen, Peter, 164
Samuels, Leslie and Fan, 127, 128, 129
San Remo Apartments, 138
Saragossa Apartments, 21
Savage, Marmion, 13, 15
Sayão, Bidú, 35
Schinasi, Morris, residence, 86, 88
Schipa, Tito, 35
School for Social Research campus, 147
School of Journalism, Columbia University, 165
Schwab, Charles M., 86
Schwab, Charles M., residence, 83, 86
Schwartz, Simon, 89
Schwartz & Gross, 41, 61, 88, 89, 180, 181
Scott, Sir Walter, 10, 12
Seagram Building, 102
Seligman, Mrs. Isaac Newton, 114, 115
Seligman banking house, 114
Seminole Apartments, 3
75th Street, East
    No. 14, 126
79th Street, East
    No. 66, 42
77th Street, West
    No. 44, 40, 52–55
Sevilla Apartments, 3
Sherry, Louis, 26
Shively, Dr. Henry L., 170, 171
Shively Sanitary Tenements, *see* East River Houses
Short, Bobby, 155
Short, R. Thomas, 52, 94
Shubert organization, 157, 158
Sidney, Sylvia, apartment, 168
Sills, Beverly, 137
Simon family, 90
Simonson, B. Hustace, 43
Sinclair Oil Company, 176
Singer Sewing Machine Company, 57
Sinister Street, 16
67th Street, West
    No. 1 (a.k.a. Hotel des Artistes), 40, 43–51, 52, 76)
66th Street, East
    No. 4 (a.k.a. 845 Fifth Avenue), 109
    No. 45 (a.k.a. 777 Madison Avenue), 52, 91–93
Sloan, John, 142
Sloan and Nast, 142, 143, 144
Smith, Henry Atterbury, 170, 171
Society for the Suppression of Unnecessary Noise, 86

Society of American Artists, 27
Soldiers' and Sailors' Monument (Manhattan), 33
Somerindyke farm, 145
Sommer, Sigmund, 93
Sotheby's 127, 129
Spanish Flats, *see* Central Park Apartments
Standard Oil Company, 153
Standard Plunger Elevator Company, 35
Stanlaws, Penrhyn, 76
Starkweather, Norris G., 174
Starrett and Van Vleck, 76, 110
Starrett Brothers, Inc., 124, 125
Statue of Liberty, 165
Stein, Cohen & Roth, 135
Steinway Piano Factory, 98, 100
Stern, Isaac, 90, 137
Stern, Louis, 35
Stern, Louis, mansion, 35
Stewart, James, 151
Stewart, William Rhinelander, Jr., 153
Stokes, Isaac Newton Phelps, 178, 179
Stokes, William Earl Dodge, 33, 35, 36
Stokes, William Earl Dodge, Jr., 35
Strakosch, Maurice, 26
Strakosch, Max, 26
Strathmore Apartments, 83–90
Straus, Jesse Isidor, 182
Strozzi Palace, 120
Studio Building, 39, 40
Stuyvesant, Rutherford, 2
Stuyvesant Apartments, 2
Sylvia Apartments, 3

Tachau, William, 44
Tagore, Rabindranath, 26
Talbot, William Henry Fox, 15
Taylor, Alfredo S. G., 32
Taylor, Freeman, and Ely, 32
Taylor, J. H., Construction Company, 130
Taylor, John, 30, 32
Taylor family, 32
tenement-house law (1901), 98, 138, 148, 162, 170
Tennessee Apartments, 4
Thaw, Harry K., 64
Third Avenue Elevated Railway, 26
Thomas, Dylan, 17
Thomas & Churchill, 93
Thursby, Emma, 26
Tiffany & Company building (1906), 167
Timkin, Mr. and Mrs. William R., 115
Tolosa Apartments, 21
Toscanini, Arturo, 35
Towers at London Terrace, 150
Town Hall (Louvain), 93
Trebilcock, Paul, 55
Trinity Building, 24
Trollope, Sir Anthony, 15
Trump, Donald, 33, 164
Trump Tower, 150
Tudor City, 134
Tuscany Apartments, 142
Tuthill, William B., 88
21st Street, East
    No. 123, 64
    No. 125, 64
23rd Street, West
    No. 429, 148

Uffizi Palace, 120
Upstairs Downstairs, 180

Valencia Apartments, 21
Valentino, Rudolph, 49
Van den Heuval, John C., mansion, 58, 59
Vanderbilt, Commodore Cornelius, 103, 177
Vanderbilt, Gloria, 153, 155, 156

Vanderbilt, Harold S., 155
Vanderbilt, Mrs. William Kissam, Sr., 170, 171
Vanderbilt, Mrs. William Kissam, Sr. foundation, 170, 172
Vanderbilt, Mrs. William Kissam, II, 125, 126, 127
Vanderbilt, Mrs. William Kissam, II apartment, 125–126
Vanderbilt, Mrs. William Kissam, II, town house, 126
Vanderbilt family, 153
Vanderbilt Tenements, *see* East River Houses
van Vleck, Charles, 115
Van Wyck, Robert A., 77
Vaux, Calvert, 74
Venice Apartments, 3
Versailles Apartments, 3
Vicious, Sid, 17
Victoria, Queen, 48, 49
Vietor, Dr. John Adolf, 115
Viollet-le-Duc, Eugène-Emmanuel, 54
"Visit from St. Nicholas, A," 145
Vivian Beaumont Theater, 127

Walden School, 68
Waldorf Towers, 127
Waldrop's Court (Edinburgh), 10
Walker, Alva, 135
Wanaque Apartments, 3
Waramaug Apartments, 3
Ware, James Edward, 6, 27, 29, 144
Ware, William R., 39
Warren & Wetmore, 105
Washington, George, 4, 63
Washington Apartments, 4
Watmough, Richard, 148
Waumbek Apartments, 3
Weaver, S. Fullerton, 105
Weekes, H. Hobart, 61
Weeks, Louis, 97
Wellington Square (London), 63
Wells, James N., 145
"Western View of the New York Apartment House, A," 108
Westminster Apartments, 3
While the Sun Shines, 15
White, Stanford, 64, 65, 68, 167, 168
White, Stanford, residence, 64, 66
White, W. Fletcher, 113
White, William A., & Sons, 150
Whitney, Cornelius Vanderbilt, 153
Whitney family, 153
Wilde, Oscar, 15
Williams, Terrance R., 173
Wilson, Woodrow, 115
Winchell, Walter, 164
Windemere Apartments, 3
Windsor Apartments, 3
Wolsey, Cardinal, 120
Woodlawn Cemetery, 167
Woollcott, Alexander, 49
Woolworth Building, 176
Worden, Helen, 105
Wurts Brothers, 93
Wynne, Henry R., 74
Wyoming Apartments, 4, 98, 100

Yale University, 63
Yellin, Samuel, 120
"Yellow Kid, The," 165
York and Sawyer, 125

Zabar, Lori, 35, 36
Zelnick, Simon, 144
Ziegfeld, Florenz, 35
Zucker, Adolph, 119
Zucker, Alfred, 161